fastread
INVESTING

fastread
INVESTING

Understand Stocks, Bonds, Mutual Funds, and more!

Rich Mintzer

Adams Media Corporation

Holbrook, Massachusetts

product manager: Chris Ciaschini
series editor: William McNeill
production director: Susan Beale
production coordinator: Debbie Sidman
layout and graphics: Arlene Apone, Paul Beatrice,
Colleen Cunningham,
Daria Perreault

Published by
Adams Media Corporation
260 Center Street, Holbrook, MA 02343, U.S.A.
www.adamsmedia.com

ISBN: 1-58062-383-X

Printed in Canada

J I H G F E D C B A

Library of Congress Cataloging-in-Publication Data available
upon request from the publisher.

This publication is designed to provide accurate and authoritative information
with regard to the subject matter covered. It is sold with the understanding that
the publisher is not engaged in rendering legal, accounting, or other professional
advice. If legal advice or other expert assistance is required, the services of a
competent professional person should be sought.
—From a *Declaration of Principles* jointly adopted by a
Committee of the American Bar Association and a
Committee of Publishers and Associations

This book is available at quantity discounts for bulk purchases.
For information, call 1-800-872-5627.

Visit our exciting home page at www.fastread.com

contents

introduction

More and more families are finding that they are now able to put a little more money aside, and that has led to an investing frenzy of sorts in recent years. Stocks—and particularly mutual funds—once thought of as investment vehicles for the "elite," are now accessible to the masses thanks to the ease at which they can be purchased and the proliferation of home computers.

No longer is putting money away in a savings account the way of the typical American family. Today, the average family, the hardworking young college graduate, the senior citizen, and both the white-collar and the blue-collar worker have the opportunity to make their money grow.

We are now a society featuring a growing number of investors, wisely trying to plan for their own future and that of their families. Investing need not be in the glamorous high-risk investments that are creating a stir in financial circles but may be a simple 401(k) plan at work, a money market mutual fund, or the old standard U.S. savings bonds. The bottom line is that more Americans are investing than ever before.

If you are successfully managing your finances to provide for yourself and/or your family, investing represents a real opportunity to make your money grow. Through investing, you take the money left after your necessary living expenses and put it to work for you to earn even more money

To invest, you will need to look at where you want to be in one, three, five, 10, and 25 years. For more risky investors the future might be the next 48 hours, but for most investors the future lies in the coming years. Because of the wide range of individual goals and dreams, and because your needs and those of your neighbors differ, your investment strategy has to be right for no one else but you. Therefore, prepared strategies and formulas don't always work. One person's financial plan and long-range goals and needs may be far more complicated than those of another person, which is why boilerplate financial planning does not work. This is why your investment plan is a personal decision.

Prior to investing, it's important that you:

1.   Are not in debt beyond fundamental things like a mortgage and perhaps a car loan
2.   Have some money already safely tucked away in accessible cash vehicles

3. Have money that is available to you specifically in case of emergency (Never invest your last dollar.)
4. Have a basic understanding of the different kinds of investments and the risks associated with those investments

Be prepared to be invested for some time and not expect instant returns. Impulsiveness doesn't usually work when it comes to investing. If you're looking for instant returns, bet on a racehorse. If you're looking to invest, buy a racehorse.

chapter one

Welcome to the Wide World of Investing

We invest to make life in the future, for ourselves, our children, our parents, and our significant others, easier. Investing wisely can also provide financial security—an important safety net in a rapidly changing world filled with uncertainty.

Investing is far from an exact science, which explains why the words "speculation" or the phrases "anticipated earnings" or "potential growth" are used. You, as an investor, have to take time for research and analysis, plus some intuitive thinking. You need to make informed decisions and have the tolerance and patience to find out if your choices were correct. There are a number of moves and strategies that you can make to safeguard your investments and to set the wheels in motion toward reaching your goals. However, there are also factors that remain out of your hands, such as sudden economic turns brought on by domestic news events, overseas events, and other circumstances that are unforeseen. This explains why even the "forecasters" take a financial bath from time to time. The element of luck is part of investing no matter how you slice it. However, this doesn't mean that you are entering rocky waters and are in danger. It simply means that you should go into investing with your eyes open and with an understanding that you should not beat yourself up if all does not go as planned.

Anyone and everyone can invest. Newcomers are joining the investment world in great numbers thanks to online trading and other technology. And many are seeing marvelous returns. You, too, can be part of the successful investing world. It does not take an extensive knowledge of Wall Street or a large bankroll to watch your money grow. You can do it with a little effort, some patience, and an ounce of good fortune.

Investing in Stocks, Bonds, and Mutual Funds

Stocks, bonds, and mutual funds are the three primary investment tools for the majority of investors looking to earn money outside of bank accounts. Even retirement accounts and college funds use these as the basis for much of their portfolios. At a basic level, stocks, bonds, and mutual funds are not particularly difficult to understand, nor do they require exorbitant sums of money. They are also easily accessible to purchase, to sell, and to follow thanks to computers, the financial media, and the Internet. There are numerous other investment options, such as real estate and commodities, but for the average investor, these are quite risky and far more complicated.

Compared to bank accounts, stocks, bonds, and mutual funds tend to provide a far greater percentage of yield. This means, in short, that your money will grow much more quickly. Bank accounts may be earning at a rate of 3 percent, while common stocks over 10 years (on the average) will earn more than twice that amount. Bond yields may see 5 percent, 7 percent, or even more, depending on the type and grade of the bond. Tech stocks such as Yahoo, Intel, and other Internet issues have seen unheard of gains, making people with modest investments wealthy in a matter of a couple of years.

Investment Smarts

When it comes to investing, you might be on the naive side now, but it doesn't mean you can't learn some basic investing smarts. It's important that you understand some of the basics. Here are a few key investment concepts for you to review.

Asset Allocation

According to a study in the *Financial Analysts Journal* in 1991, only 7 percent of successful investing depends upon the selection of specific stocks, bonds, or mutual funds. The other 93 percent of successful investing depends upon selecting the right asset classes in which to be invested, as well as when to be invested in them. The question of whether you should be invested in CDs, the stock market, the bond market, real estate, money market funds, precious metals, global investments, and so on is, therefore, the tantamount question that precedes which mutual fund or stock to buy.

Within the broad grouping of asset classes (stocks, bonds, mutual funds, etc.) there are more specific asset classes. For example, equity (stock) mutual funds include large-cap stocks, medium or mid-cap stocks, and small-cap stocks ("caps" equate to the size of the company in regard to their assets), plus various sectors such as utilities, technologies, energy, and financial. There are cyclical stocks, and a host of industries such as the auto industry, airline industry, and so on. Each of these sectors and industries can be defined as a different asset class with very different behavioral characteristics. The stocks within that asset class will most often behave according to how that asset class is doing as a whole more than according to the fundamentals of a particular stock or bond. If, for example, IBM reports below-expectation earnings, then (in most cases) so will Apple, Intel, and the entire industry, unless there is a particular story centering around IBM, such as a merger or lawsuit, etc. The same holds true with funds. Asset classes perform in specific ways, the most notable being the tech stocks and tech stock funds of recent years. Surely, you can find an Internet stock that is the exception to the rule, but by and large, the sector has grown universally.

Asset allocation, therefore, means determining how much of your assets you are putting into each kind of asset class. You will ultimately allocate your assets into stocks and/or equity funds, bonds and/or bond funds, money market funds, or other types of investment vehicles based on the following factors:

1. Income level
2. Amount of money you have available to invest
3. Level of investing sophistication
4. Ultimate use for the investment, or goal (retirement, college, etc.)
5. Age
6. Time frame until reaching your goal
7. Level of risk/tolerance

But how do you distribute them?

Generally, as investors get closer to their goals, they will become more conservative, particularly if money is earmarked for retirement. Approaching retirement, many investors will put a higher percentage of assets into safer investments with lower fundamental risk. The thinking is often that if you lower your amount of assets in equities and switch to bonds and cash instruments as you approach retirement, you will have a steady flow of income with less risk.

Another theory, however, would be that since over the long term the stock market has always done well (and the average life span may be 20 years beyond a retirement at age 65), you might be just as well off keeping a reasonably high percentage in stocks (equities). The equities will grow, and if you should need income you can always sell a stock. Retirees need not invest so conservatively that the money is no longer growing over the next 20 or even 30 years. Retirees today need a certain amount for living expenses and various wants and needs, so that part is invested in a more conservative vehicle. Beyond that, the approach may be somewhat more aggressive to build up money for the next generation.

The theories vary, but the main idea is to allocate your assets in line with the factors mentioned here and remember that everyone's situation is different. Do not let financial planners talk you into more-or-less conservative investments that are not right for your personal needs.

Some Suggestions

While I can't emphasize enough that your investment strategy must be based on your individual needs and goals, we still offer a few *broad* portfolio planning strategies for allocating your funds. These are merely a few allocation breakdowns to give you a ballpark look at what you could do in various situations, tailoring them to meet your needs, income, age, etc.

1. If you have a long-term plan, with a 10- to 15-year goal, you might start with a more aggressive approach to asset allocation, going with at least 85 to 90 percent in equities, including 25 percent in an international fund and 20 percent in emerging growth funds or small-cap companies.

2. If your goals are coming up in seven to 10 years, such as having a child in grade school and saving for college, you can still be somewhat aggressive, with a small amount of international holdings as part of an 80-20 or 75-25 equity-bond split. You can balance your bond fund between conservative and aggressive bonds or bond funds and have some cash investments as well.

3. If you are looking at reaching your goals in four to seven years, such as having a high-school-aged

child heading for college, you may want to lean toward an even split between safer bond investments and equities. In this case, however, you should be opting to invest in more established companies (even some that pay dividends) rather than going for the higher-risk stocks.

4.   If you are reaching retirement, it's usually, though not always, the time to go in the low-risk safe direction. A 75-25 split with bonds leading the way may be the right approach. Once you've established a safe, income-producing portfolio, however, unless you are adverse to risk, you can use the last 5 to 10 percent to play with a riskier equity fund.

Risk/Tolerance

Some people keep their money in a vault and visit it so infrequently that they barely remember the combination. Others make frequent deposits into the slot machines in Las Vegas and Atlantic City. How risky you choose to be with your money is part and parcel to your personality. Risk means taking a chance, with the outcome not guaranteed to be in your favor. In life, most things require some degree of risk, no matter how minimal. Financially, you can lose money. Your tolerance is how comfortable you will feel with an unfavorable outcome. When we take greater risks we need to know from the onset that the chance of losing money is greater. However, the rewards are usually greater too.

Risk versus tolerance is one of the first determinants in how you should invest your money. It is a way to assess which investment route you wish to take: conservative or aggressive.

Some investors will take much bigger risks looking for large gains, while others are content just having their money earn them a steady income. There are levels in between.

Your life situation will be a factor in what level of investment risk you choose to take. For example, you might seek out a higher-risk investment when putting money into a college fund when your child is three or four years of age. At this point you can build up funds more quickly since you have more time to adjust should the investments not be performing as you had hoped. However, once your son or daughter is four or five years from college, you may want to move your money into more sure-fire, lower-risk (lower reward) investments for safety. The level of risk you choose, therefore, depends on your financial goals and how much time you have to meet such goals.

An unmarried, 29-year-old corporate executive may have more money available to put into riskier investments than the married father or mother of three paying a mortgage and high living expenses. The executive is most likely at a point where his or her money can grow without drastically affecting long-term plans. When it comes to risk/tolerance, there is no real formula unless you factor in all the components: age, income, savings, goals, and personality.

Liquidity

Liquidity is a way of asking, *How fast can I get out of my investment and have the cash should I need it?* When you have money in your bank account or in a money market account, it is accessible to you and therefore "liquid."

Stocks, mutual funds, and even most bonds are liquid in that you are not locked into them with a penalty of losing money as you would be with a CD or 401(k). When you sell a stock, fund, or bond (or redeem a bond), there is usually a short wait of a few days or perhaps a week until you see your check. If you plan accordingly, as advised here, and have some money set aside in cash instruments, you should not worry about the liquidity of this type of investing. The more worrisome investments, in terms of liquidity, would be areas such as owning real estate or dealing in fine art, where your only way of becoming liquid is to find a buyer. These are not savvy investments for the rookie investor.

If you are properly insured for your life situation (home owners' insurance if you own a home, and so on), you will be covered for major emergencies. In reality, you can still sell off a stock and probably see the money faster than you'll see the check from the insurance company. Having money available for emergencies is one aspect of liquidity. However, the other side is knowing when you are going to need the money. For example, if you know you are buying a house in the near future, you will want to have money liquid for the down payment. If you are approaching a down payment and are worried that a drop in the market will eat into the money you need for that down payment, then you should move your money into a money market fund. Returning to asset allocation, you want a portion of your allocated investments to be liquid. This is usually the case with most of the "traditional" investment options.

Returns

Closely tied with risk are returns. Traditionally, greater risk means greater potential returns. You can see a return on your investment in the form of a dividend, from interest, or from capital gains due to making a sale of shares of a fund, stock, bond, or other investment vehicle. Compare returns you can make from various investments based on the returns such investments have seen in the past, over several years. Short-term returns are hard to gauge as they can be based on a sudden event or turn in the market.

Interest from bonds, as well as bank accounts or CDs, offer a steady (safe) way to see a return on your money. Your principal remains steady while your money grows. Preferred stocks and some common stocks will pay dividends whereby you will get a steady, although not glamorous, return on your investment. As long as the money is growing faster than the rate of inflation, this is a way of seeing a "comfortable" return.

Your level of risk/tolerance will enter the picture as you determine which investment is right for you. It's also worth noting that you do not have to fall into only one category. Many investors are receiving interest and/or dividends while holding stocks or mutual funds that pay neither but are growing steadily in value. They are bringing in high returns, or money back on your dollar, which can be turned into a profit when you sell.

It is worth noting that many investment planners and counselors will agree that chasing high returns is not generally considered a good investment strategy. Yesterday's high returns will not necessarily be the high returns of tomorrow. And, most often, significant returns take time to build, through compounding interest, or through being in the stock market for several years. Rather than chase returns, you will almost always be better off setting up your goals and following a set plan of action that has you allocating your money into different asset classes and diversifying within each asset class, which brings us to the next area, "diversification."

Diversification

To diversify means to "spread it around" or "not put all your eggs in one basket." In the world of investing, there are several investment vehicles available; you need not choose only one. Among the reasons why mutual funds are so popular these days is that they select several stocks, bonds, or other investment vehicles for you. Funds are managed by professional money managers who choose a variety of investment vehicles. In short, they diversify.

Owning a mutual fund does not mean you cannot also own stocks, bonds, or more than one fund. Tantamount to putting money on seven numbers on the roulette table instead of just one, you have better odds at winning. However, unlike the roulette wheel, which will have just one winning number per spin, you could win on several stocks.

The most prominent strategy is to mix high- and low-risk investment vehicles and to allocate the assets wisely. Once your funds are allocated into different asset groups, you diversify within that asset group. One of the biggest mistakes an investor can make is putting everything in one pot.

Commissions and Costs

The primary cost associated with investing is that of paying commissions. Whether you are trading online or dealing with a real human being, commission fees will be attached to stock transactions. Mutual funds can be "no-loads," which means you do not pay a commission. However, there are operating costs associated with mutual funds. Many people don't bother to examine the operating costs associated with their mutual funds. Sometimes they can eat away at your profits, so they are worth checking out. Brokers dealing bonds will buy them at one price and sell them to you at another. The difference, or the spread, is in essence a commission of sorts for the broker. Buying government bonds on your own can eliminate this "spread."

The Intimidation Factor

There are three reasons why many people do not invest: they do not have the extra funds, they do not know what to do, and they are intimidated, which is often linked to not knowing enough about investing. This book will hopefully alleviate the last two reasons. You do not need to know all the buzzwords to be able to put your money into a stock, bond, or mutual fund and have it work for you. You do, however, need to know the basics:

> What investing is all about
> What to look for when selecting an investment
> How to follow your portfolio
> How to position yourself for better results to
>   meet your goals
> How to get out when you choose to

The moral is to stay on top of your investments. Make sure they are where you want them to be.

chapter two

Investing: Getting In, Patience, and Getting Out

Now that you have determined your financial goals, armed yourself with investment "smarts," determined how much risk you could tolerate, and accepted that your investment growth will not happen overnight, what do you do?

It's important to know three things: "Getting In," "Patience," and "Getting Out." In the previous section we discussed areas such as asset allocation, diversification, liquidity, and risk/tolerance. As we approach the "ins and outs" of actually investing, it's important to see how these areas tie together and how "risk" can be broken down into various types of risks while building your portfolio. Building a portfolio from the ground up will give you the investment edge you need to best position yourself to:

1. Manage away risk.
2. Seek returns.

Interestingly enough, many investors look at #2 before #1. Brokers get commissions from selling you on #2, and although they will discuss #1, they are focused on seducing you with #2.

If you choose to build a portfolio, however, you will see the increasing value of #1. Often as we mature as investors, we begin to look at protecting ourselves. Safety becomes more significant than chasing the big reward.

Risks in Detail

A good investment strategy begins with managing away, as best you can, six types of risk: four investment risks and two risks that will affect your investment strategies as well.

Fundamental Risk

Fundamental risk, or business risk, is often (combined with technical risk) the primary risk referred to when risk is discussed. Fundamental risk applies to bonds, stocks, real estate, and all investments. It is the risk inherent within a particular business enterprise that relates to the company's financial strains, their position in the marketplace, their reputation, how they fare against their competition, and so on.

The best way to manage your portfolio to minimize the effects of fundamental risk is to diversify. This is where you are investing in different companies in different industries within the same asset class.

Technical Risk

Technical risk involves measuring things such as unemployment, interest rates, the budget deficit, and various other economic and market indicators. All of these external factors play a part in the success or failure of your investment. Technical risk, also known as market risk, is how well the market of your investment fares in regard to these factors. The affects on the overall market will affect your investment—which brings us back to the all ships rise or sink with the tide analogy.

Managing technical risk means having a balanced portfolio. This is another way of diversifying across asset groups by having your dollars allocated into stocks, bonds, real estate, money market funds, CDs, and so on. If you plan to spread your money across various markets and asset classes, you can lessen technical or market risk before focusing on the specific investments within each group.

Interest Rate Risk

Interest rate risk is how your investment is responding to the direction in which the interest rate is heading and how fast the rate is going. Often people assume that this only affects the bond market. This is not true. There is strong correlation between interest rate risk and the stock market. While stocks have various other factors that directly affect them, they will frequently follow suit with bonds and react in the same inverse manner to the direction in which the interest rate moves.

You can manage away interest rate risk by having part of your portfolio in fixed principal investments with a guaranteed interest rate. Also, having a portion of your portfolio leaning toward short-term bonds (rather than long-term bonds, which will fluctuate more) will help you better avoid interest rate risk.

Inflation Risk

Inflation risk is the risk that inflation will rise faster than your investment and that your dollars will be worth less in the future than they are today. In an effort to manage away inflation risk, or purchasing power risk, you need to look at stocks, real estate, and investments that will, over time, beat the inflation rate. During periods of moderate or low inflation the stock market performs well. During periods of high inflation the market can fall dramatically. It's hard to beat high inflation risk, but you can ride it out with investments that have a tendency to stay ahead of the projected inflation rate.

For this reason, it's also important to gauge appropriately when looking ahead in retirement accounts. Many people do not factor in inflation. There's no way to know what the inflation rate will be in 20 years, but always remember to include it along with taxes (in investments that are taxed) to see if you are coming out ahead.

Liquidity Risk

Liquidity risk is technically not considered an investment risk; it is not a risk based on the investment itself but on how much you need to be liquid. It is the risk that we will need our capital at a time other than we planned for. It deals with the risk of being able to rapidly convert our assets into cash.

Money market funds are the low end of liquidity risk, and actual real-estate investments along with locking money into retirement plans such as IRAs and 401(k)s are on the high end of liquidity risk. The best way to manage against the potential problem is simply to determine how much money you need in your budget for a certain time period, be it weekly or monthly, and make sure you always have that money available to you plus some reserve.

Tax Risk

Tax risk is also not considered an investment risk; like liquidity risk, it isn't a risk to the actual investment, but more to the investor. You know ahead of time which investments are taxable and which are not. It is important to determine where you will land in the "tax bracket" game, and try to determine accordingly if some (and there aren't many) tax-free investment vehicles are a plus for your portfolio.

Most of the investment tax management, however, does not come from the investment itself, but rather from the vehicle in which the investments are made. IRAs, 401(k)s or 403(b)s, and variable life insurance are vehicles in which you make investments. The structure provides you tax-exemption or deferral to an extent dictated by the vehicle as well as by state tax laws. Often a tax-exempt or deferred vehicle directed at retirement also falls under the "not very liquid" heading. Nonetheless, from a portfolio-building standpoint, it is also important to address tax risk.

Okay, enough about the portfolio, or the "big picture." Let's talk about simply starting out, or "getting in."

Getting In

Now that you're ready to get into the pool are you going slowly, step by step; jumping into the shallow end; or diving in off the high board? New investors will commonly start off small and build as they feel more comfortable. There's nothing wrong with this approach. If your initial investment doesn't perform as you hoped, it may give you a "real" indication of your risk tolerance level.

Here are some tips for getting in:

1. *Set realistic expectations for your investments.* Investing is a way of watching your money grow, and growing takes time.
2. *Start sooner than later.* Remember that money builds over time. If you are able to start investing regularly at age 35, by the time you're 65 your money will have had 30 years of appreciation. This doesn't mean you can't do very well investing in your forties or even fifties, but it's always to your advantage to give your money time to grow.
3. *Prepare to be proactive.* Managing your assets is also not solely the job of a mutual fund manager, broker, financial consultant, or anyone else. Many people who are invested in 401(k) plans or other long-term retirement plans forget that they have the flexibility to move their investments around within the plan.
4. *Just Do It!* This is not by any means saying that you should not do your homework, and is not

contradictory to the previous advice. However, it means that there is a ton of information available and at some point you have to stop investigating and (once you feel you can make an informed decision) as Nike says, "Just Do It!" You need to reach a point where you are simply ready to get into the pool.

5. *Diversify.* The idea that diversification means you need to have large sums of money invested and/or be a more savvy investor is incorrect. Mutual funds can immediately, for even $500, have your money diversified.

6. *Manage your risk.* Look at investments that best combat the risk you are concerned about, be it inflation, taxation, liquidity, or all of the above. Allocate your assets across different asset classes and try to cover the various types of risk associated with investing.

7. *Pay yourself first.* Once you've paid your monthly bills and made sure your expenses have been covered, you should then add to your investment. Having direct deposit from your paycheck makes this easier, but if it's up to you, make adding to your investment(s) a regular part of the process.

8. *Reinvest your earnings.* Many investments, including mutual funds, will do this for you, but it's to your advantage to keep your income working for you unless you need it for a specific purpose.

Patience

Although you won't hear it mentioned in the same context as "risk" or "diversify," which are investment terms, good old "patience" is a major factor in investing—one that generally works in your favor.

It has been proven repeatedly that just as retail prices go up over time, so does the stock market. Patience is not easily found on Wall Street, but it is a valuable asset if you can find it. Being patient and letting time take its course is part of wise investment planning. Just as retirement funds succeed and grow over time, so will other investments. Playing the market on the short-term basis may work for shrewd investors who follow the details of the market and the financial updates very closely, but for others it's essentially gambling. World events over the course of a few days can send the market soaring or dropping and your investment along with it.

Time is one of the best allies of most investors. Bond holders, because there is a set maturity date, are more often aware of the idea of a "time frame." There is no such comfort (no time table) when you own a stock or stock fund. Therefore, you need to make your own. Shrewd investors who work hard at following the market (stocks or bonds) and have a more calculated idea of when to buy and sell can play the investing game on a short-term basis. It is riskier, and one needs to stay very much on top of the business world to be successful. You need to look ahead at what is forthcoming in an industry, in a company, or in the market as a whole. Chasing after last year's hot stock or mutual fund generally does not work because the path of investing is to move forward and think ahead.

While looking toward the future, you need to understand that the road to your goal will not always be a smooth trip, just as you'll hit a bump or two while driving or some turbulence when flying. A company, even a solid, long-standing blue-chip company, will have an occasional quarter where their earnings are off. Some investors will jump ship; others will note the long history of success of a company and resolve that they will bounce right back with something else. Good investors will also see that many industries will have higher and lower periods. Beyond being patient, it's often to your advantage to pick up more shares of a solid company that you believe in when the stock price drops.

Tips for maintaining your PATIENCE include:

1. *Avoid impulsive reactions.* You need to give yourself "stop orders" at times to ride out the volatility associated with most investments. Don't impulsively bail out. You also should stop yourself from buying impulsively without checking up on the stock first.

2. *Stick to your goals.* If you have set up goals for yourself, to have X amount of money in X number of years, remind yourself that these goals will not be reachable without patience.

3. *Smile at advice.* Take advice with a grain of salt, smile, and listen to most well-intentioned friends, neighbors, relatives, and so on. Even the myriad of "experts" out there will have new-and-improved ways for you to invest. There's nothing wrong with investigating some advice that sounds feasible to

your goals and needs, and even making some adjustments as you go along (in fact, managing your asset allocation can be important), but you should maintain and be patient with the core of investments in your portfolio. Don't be easily swayed.

Getting Out

There is a lot of talk and a lot written about putting your money into investments. However, there isn't a lot written about taking your money out. Sure, it's easy to put money into a 401(k) or a similar plan and know that at a certain age you will be required to take the money out, but what about selling off an investment? When do you sell your shares of a stock or mutual fund? When you invest, you have three options: buy, sell, or hold. "Buying" occupies most of the magazine articles and is the basis for the advertisements for fund companies on television and in print. Buying into a fund family brings in business, and buying shares of a stock makes the stock more attractive. Selling, however, is what will transform the value of shares of stock or shares in a mutual fund into income. You can sell a bond at an attractive price, depending on the market. You can sell an investment for a profit or as a way of bailing out of a sinking ship.

Far too few investors are well-versed at selling. The two biggest mistakes, traditionally, are selling too soon and waiting too long with a losing proposition. Yes, holding onto stocks, overall, is usually to your benefit. However, that does not necessarily mean you hold onto them forever, nor does it mean that there are not exceptions to the rule. After all, if every stock went up and was a "winner," then there would be no level of risk involved, and that is not the case. Studies have shown that investors will far more quickly sell a wining stock and take the profits than accept they made a mistake and bail out of a loser. Everyone likes a good comeback story and there is always that ounce of hope that if you hang onto a sinking ship it might suddenly rise again.

General tips on GETTING OUT include:

1. *Remember why you got in.* Evaluate why you got into the investment and see if the same reasons for being in it, or equivalent reasons, would have you buying it now.

2. *Be able to admit when you've made a mistake.* Forget bravado; even the biggest investors from Warren Buffet on down have blown a few.

3. *Remember moderation.* Sell some, keep some. You can always move from the deep end of the pool toward the shallower end without getting out.

4. *Set limits.* I sell at X and celebrate, or I sell at X and drown my sorrows.

5. *Remember your goals—stay focused.* If it's time to pay that college tuition, then use the money, or at least the portion necessary. If you can now afford the dream house, take the money and buy it. There's nothing wrong with continuing to invest, but the initial goals are why you are investing.

6. *Try to gauge the future realistically.* Look for a sound basis for holding onto an investment rather than sentimentality or a hunch.

chapter three

Stock
Basics

What a Stock Represents

Before you buy stock, it's a good idea to understand exactly what that purchase represents. When you buy stock, you're actually buying a portion of a corporation. Essentially, a share of stock represents the percentage of a company you own. If a company has 200,000 shares outstanding and you own 200 shares, then you own 1/1,000 of the company. You become an official shareholder with your first stock purchase.

Once you become a common stock shareholder, you will receive quarterly and annual reports. Such reports feature a wealth of information, including new products and/or services, an earnings (gains or losses) report, and the names of key company executives. You also have voting rights with common stock ownership, usually one vote per share, and you're welcome to attend stockholders' meetings, where you can gain insight about a company's direction and about its recent performance.

Types of Stocks

Common stocks are securities, sold to the public, that constitute ownership in a corporation. When you make an investment, you will be putting your money into a "public" company, which allows you—as part of the public—to become an owner or to have equity in the company. That's why stocks are often referred to as equities.

Although it is a much less popular alternative to common stock, you can also purchase what is known as preferred stock. This type of stock has a fixed dividend and a redemption date. Income received has nothing to do with the company's earnings. If the company goes under, holders of preferred stock have priority when it comes to dividend payments. Preferred stock really is more like a junior bond, than common stock. This book will concentrate on common stock because, like its name, it's the far more common choice for stock investors.

You can invest in a mega-company or a micro-cap company that has just begun to soar. There are different categories of stock to suit almost every personality. The variety includes blue-chip, growth, small-cap, cyclical, defensive, value, income, and speculative stocks.

Large-Cap, Mid-Cap, and Small-Cap

The market value of all outstanding shares of a particular stock is synonymous with its market capitalization (or cap). Market capitalization is calculated by multiplying the market price by the number of outstanding shares. The number of outstanding shares refers to the number of shares that were sold and are, therefore, now shares outstanding. Larger companies will usually have a lot more outstanding shares than their smaller counterparts. Shares that are issued are outstanding until they are redeemed, reacquired, converted, or canceled.

A public company with 20 million shares outstanding that trade at $40 each would have a market capitalization of $800 million. Although there are no concrete rules to categorize stocks, they can be differentiated by the following:

Large-cap: $5 billion and over
Mid-cap: Between $1 billion and $5 billion
Small-cap: Between $300 million and $1 billion
Micro-cap: Below $300 million

Blue-Chip Stocks

These are considered to be the most prestigious, well-established companies that are publicly traded, many of which have practically become household names. Included in this mostly large-cap mix are IBM (NYSE: IBM), Disney (NYSE: DIS), and Coca-Cola (NYSE: KO). A good number of blue-chip companies have been in existence for more than 25 years and are still leading the pack in their respective industries.

Since most of these organizations have a solid track record, they are good investment vehicles for individuals leaning to the conservative side when stock picking.

Growth Stocks

As the name suggests, growth stocks comprise companies that have strong growth potential. Many companies in this category have sales, earnings, and market share that are growing faster than the overall economy. Such stocks, which currently include such companies as Lucent Technologies (NYSE: LU), and Cisco (NASDAQ: CSCO), usually represent companies that are big on research and development. Earnings in these companies are usually put right back into the business. Growth stocks may be riskier than their blue-chip counterparts, but in many cases you can also reap greater rewards. Pioneers in new technology are often growth stock companies. In recent years, growth stocks have outperformed value stocks (defined later in this section). That has not been the case at times in the past, and the trend may well turn around in the future.

Cyclical Stocks

Companies with earnings that are strongly tied to the business cycle are considered to be cyclical. When the economy picks up momentum, these stocks follow this positive trend. When the economy slows down, these stocks follow, too.

Defensive Stocks

No matter how the market is faring, defensive stocks are relatively stable under most economic conditions. Stocks with this characteristic include food companies, drug manufacturers, and utility companies. For the most part, you can't live without these products no matter what the economic climate may be at any given time.

Value Stocks

Such stocks look inexpensive when compared to earnings, dividends, sales, or other fundamental factors. When there is a big run on growth stocks, value stocks may be ignored. However, many investors believe that value stocks are a good deal given their reasonable price in relation to many growth stocks. Warren Buffet would probably vouch for that.

Income Stocks

Income stocks may fit the bill if generating income is your primary goal. One example of an income stock is public utility companies because such stocks have traditionally paid higher dividends than other types of stock. As with any stock, it's wise to look for a solid company with a good track record.

Speculative Stocks

Any company that's boasting about their brilliant ideas but doesn't have the earnings and revenue to back it up would be classified as a speculative stock. Since these companies have yet to prove their true worth, they are a risky investment. Speculative stocks include many internet companies that don't yet have earnings.

Penny Stocks

Penny stocks are stocks that sell for five dollars or less and, in many cases, you're lucky if they're worth even that much. Most penny stocks usually have no substantial income or revenue. You have a high potential for loss with penny stocks.

The Stock Market

Several markets make up what is known as "the stock market." Many stocks are traded on the New York Stock Exchange (NYSE), the National Association of Securities Dealers Automated Quotations (NASDAQ), and the American Stock Exchange (Amex). In addition, such cities as Boston, Chicago, Philadelphia, Denver, San Francisco, and Los Angeles have exchanges. You can also find exchanges in major international cities like London and Tokyo.

Also known as "The Big Board," the New York Stock Exchange is home to the most prominent players like IBM, AOL, and Disney. Among other requirements, a company must have at least 1.1 million public shares of stock outstanding, must show pretax income of at least $6.5 million over the three most recent fiscal years (each year has to be equal to or more than the previous year), and the company's market value of public shares must be at least $40 million to be on board. In addition, the company's most recent year's pretax income must be at least $2.5 million, and its net tangible assets must be a minimum of $40 million.

The National Association of Security Dealers Automated Quotations (NASDAQ) and the American Stock Exchange (Amex) united in October 1998, creating the NASDAQ/Amex Market Group. The American Stock Exchange is now a subsidiary of the National Association of Securities Dealers,

Inc. (NASD). However, the NASDAQ and the Amex are still currently operating as separate entities. NASDAQ is an over-the-counter (OTC) market, which is the term used to describe securities that are traded through telephone and computer networks as opposed to through an auction exchange.

Stock Market Indexes

The *Dow Jones Industrial Average* is the most prominent stock index in the world. The 30 stocks on the Dow, which are all part of the New York Stock Exchange, are established blue-chip companies like McDonald's, Coca-Cola, DuPont, and Eastman Kodak. Companies on the Dow Jones Industrial Average, which was created to mimic the United States stock market as a whole, represent a variety of market segments such as entertainment, automotive, healthcare products, and financial services. General Electric is the only company that was included in the original Dow Jones Industrial Average created in 1896 that is still part of its makeup today.

The stocks currently in the Dow Jones Industrial Average are:

1. Alcoa Inc. (AA)
2. American Express Co. (AXP)
3. AT&T Corp. (T)
4. Boeing Co. (BA)
5. Caterpillar Inc. (CAT)
6. Citigroup Inc. (C)
7. Coca-Cola Co. (KO)

8. E. I. du Pont de Nemours and Company (DD)
9. Eastman Kodak Co. (EK)
10. Exxon Mobil Corp. (XOM)
11. General Electric Co. (GE)
12. General Motors Corp. (GM)
13. Hewlett-Packard Co. (HWP)
14. Honeywell International Inc. (HON)
15. Home Depot Inc (HD).
16. Intel Corporation (INTC)
17. International Business Machines Corp. (IBM)
18. International Paper Co. (IP)
19. Johnson and Johnson (JNJ)
20. J.P. Morgan and Co. (JPM)
21. McDonald's Corp. (MCD)
22. Merck and Co. (MRK)
23. Microsoft Corporation (MFST)
24. Minnesota Mining and Manufacturing Co. (MMM)
25. Philip Morris Co. (MO)
26. Procter & Gamble Co. (PG)
27. SBC Communications Inc. (SBC)
28. United Technologies (UTX)
29. Walt Disney Company (DIS)
30. Wal-Mart Stores Inc. (WMT)

The *Standard & Poor's 500 Index* is a benchmark that is widely used by professional stock investors. The Index represents 500 stocks—400 industrial stocks, 20 transportation stocks, 40 utility stocks, and 40 financial stocks. It consists primarily of stocks listed on the New York Stock Exchange, although it also features stocks that are a part of the

American Stock Exchange (Amex) and over-the-counter (OTC) stocks.

The *Russell 2000* was created to be a comprehensive representation of the U.S. small-cap equities market. It measures the performance of the smallest 2,000 companies in the Russell 3000 Index.

Initial Public Offerings (IPOs)

When a company chooses to "go public," that means they are issuing stocks to the public at large. Looking to grow, they sell shares of stock to raise capital without creating debt. Investors, in turn, expect to earn profits by purchasing stock in such a company. An initial public offering (IPO) is held when a company issues stock for the first time.

The detailed process of issuing stock is usually done through an investment bank, with which a company works to determine how much capital is needed, the price of the stock, how much it will cost to issue such equities, and so forth. A company must file a registration statement with the Securities and Exchange Commission (SEC), which carefully investigates the company to ensure that it has made full disclosure in compliance with the Securities Act of 1933. The SEC will then determine whether or not the company has met all the criteria to issue common stock, or "go public."

Prior to the stock going public, the SEC must make sure that everything is in order (this can take some time), and a red herring is usually issued, which is a prospectus informing the public about the company and the impending stock offering.

When the stock is ready to "go public," a stock price is issued in accordance with the current market.

The best way to find out about an IPO is to have a broker who has a pulse on all breaking financial news. *Investment Dealer's Digest* lists all IPOs that are registered with the SEC. Once the stock is issued, the publication gives you an IPO update. Companies awaiting an IPO will often call the leading brokerage houses and/or brokers they are familiar with who will inform their clients about such an offering. They are looking for investors who will hold onto the stock for some time. As is the case with anything new, these stocks can be very risky due to their potentially volatile nature. It's a good idea to wait until the stock settles before you determine whether it would be a viable investment. The vast majority of stocks that you will be researching have probably already been actively trading.

The Securities and Exchange Commission (SEC)

The Securities and Exchange Commission (SEC) was created after the Great Depression to regulate the securities industry as a whole. The SEC oversees the industry to ensure that no illegal activity is being conducted. In addition, the organization sets many standards for both brokers and investors. Companies trading on stock exchanges nationwide must be registered with the SEC.

Insider information is one of the issues reviewed by the SEC. Essentially, insider information (also known as insider trading) deals with the buying and selling of stock based on confidential information obtained from an "inside" source not available to the rest of the public. The SEC also oversees trading activity to ensure that investors are getting the appropriate prices when both buying and selling securities.

The SEC requires that publicly traded companies publish regular financial reports. The reports provided to the SEC are called Form 10K or Form 10Q for annual or quarterly reports, respectively.

chapter four

Selecting, Buying, and Selling Stocks

Buy What You Know

We're all consumers, most of us with very distinct preferences when it comes to certain products and services. If you've found a consistently great product or service, odds are that you're not alone in your discovery. The stocks of superior companies that have stood the test of time are always in great demand.

Familiarity takes a lot of the anxiety out of picking stocks. It also gives you valuable insight about honing in on a specific company. In addition to your own experiences, observations are another way to gain valuable insight. During your recent trip to Japan, did you notice people consuming huge quantities of Coca-Cola? While waiting to pay for dinner at the local restaurant, did many of the patrons pull out American Express cards?

By being an informed consumer, you already have a better grasp of the market than you may realize. You probably have stock preferences and a better understanding of the business world than you would have guessed. However, knowledge of a given product or service is just the beginning of the process.

Know the Basics

Purchasing shares of stock is a lot like buying a business. That's the way Warren Buffet, one of the world's most successful investors, views it—and his philosophy is certainly worth noting! If you wouldn't want to own the entire company, then you should think twice before you consider buying even a piece of it. If you think of investing in these terms, you'll probably be a lot more cautious when singling out a specific company.

Most people wouldn't buy a business without conducting a thorough investigation of every aspect of the company. It's important to become acquainted with all of the details. What are all of the products and services the company offers? Which part of the business accounts for the greatest revenue? Is the company too diversified? Who are its competitors? Is there a demand for the company's offerings? Is the company an industry leader? Is there an experienced, innovative, and progressive management team? Are any mergers and acquisitions in the works? Until you understand exactly what the company does and how well it does it, it would be wise to postpone your decision to rush into an investment.

It's a good idea to continue your research efforts by reviewing the following factors:

Earnings per share. Earnings per share is the company's net income divided by the number of common shares outstanding. It is the company's profit. Growth rate is often determined in terms of earnings per share. Finding a company with a strong earning growth is advisable. You also want to review the company's earnings per share over the past several years to see if the company is growing on a consistent basis.

Price/earnings ratio (P/E). Reviewing a company's price/earnings ratio is an integral part of the stock selection decision-making process. A P/E ratio is the stock price divided by the earnings per share. Essentially, it tells you how much investors are willing to pay for one dollar of the company's earnings. Since every industry has its own unique qualities, you want to find out what the average P/E is for that sector. A P/E of 20 means that investors are paying 20 times earnings for the stock.

Book value. Shareholder's equity is another term for book value. Book value is defined as the company's assets minus its liabilities. The number you get from this equation is then divided by the number of shares outstanding. Many experts say you should look for a low stock price relative to the book value per share. This is how you find "value" stocks selling at less than book value.

Price volatility. Price volatility is often measured by beta. Beta shows you how a stock is moving in relation to changes in the Standard & Poor's 500 Stock Index. The index is fixed at 1.00. Therefore, a stock with a beta of 2 moves up and down two times as much as the Standard & Poor's Index.

Dividends. Dividends are payments to shareholders that are not based on the stock price but are made simply because the company has reaped healthy profits and chooses to reward shareholders. Depending on the company's profits, the board of directors will decide whether to initiate a dividend to shareholders, as well as how often and when these dividends will be paid. Dividends are usually most important to investors looking for income (hence income stocks).

Find out the current dividend and compare it with the dividend rate for the past five years. When a company's primary goal is growth, dividends may be small—or nonexistent. Usually stock dividends are paid by large-scale companies.

Number of shares outstanding. Shares outstanding refers to the number of shares issued to the general public, including company employees. It's a good idea to start your investing career by looking at companies with at least 5 million shares outstanding, because this indicates that the stock is heavily traded and, as a result, will not be difficult to sell if you should take that course of action.

Total return. The total return on a stock makes it possible for you to compare your stock investments with similar types of investments, such as corporate or municipal bonds, treasuries, mutual funds, and unit investment trusts. To calculate the total returns, add (or subtract) the stock's price change and dividends for the past 12 months and then divide by the price at the beginning of the 12-month period. For example, suppose you buy a stock at $42 per share and receive $2.50 in dividends for the next 12-month period. At the end of the period, you sell the stock at $45. Your calculations would look like this:

Dividend: $2.50
Price appreciation: +$3.00 per share
$2.50 + $3.00 per share =$5.50
$5.50 divided by $42.00 = 13 percent
Your total return is a 13 percent increase.

Technical or Fundamental Analysis?

Investors generally follow one of two stock-picking techniques: fundamental analysis or technical analysis. Technical analysis relies on charts and graphs to determine stock movements. Fundamental analysis is the more commonly used method for beginning investors. It includes both growth and value investing.

Technical analysis involves charts and graphs containing information about past stock price patterns. Essentially, these are patterns that followers of technical analysis may use when investing. There are a number of patterns such analysts recognize to be historically recurring. The trick is to identify the pattern before it is completed. However, it's not as easy and clear-cut as one might be led to believe. Those who utilize this technique believe that you can forecast future stock prices by studying past price trends. Therefore, they buy and sell stock based on stock price movements. Such individuals tend to buy and sell stocks on a much more frequent basis than individuals who use fundamental analysis when making investment decisions. Technical analysts take into account things like moving averages, trend lines, and even things like a "double top" or a "head and shoulders" pattern.

Fundamental analysis is a long-used, common way to review stocks. The technique involves an analysis of the company's ability to generate earnings and examines the value of the company's total assets. Value investing and growth investing are two subdivisions of fundamental analysis. Proponents of fundamental analysis believe that stock prices will rise as a result of growth. Earnings, dividends, and book values are all examined, and a buy-and-hold approach is usually followed. Fundamental analysis advocates maintain the view that stocks of well-run, high-quality companies will become more valuable as time unfolds.

Getting Started: On Your Own or with a Broker?

Choosing the way you will conduct your investing is an important decision. Fortunately, you have several options, each equipped with both pros and cons. However, there is no universally "correct" way to invest. Whichever way you choose to conduct your investment affairs has a lot to do with your level of investment interest and just how eager you are to partake in the entire research process.

If you are ready, willing, and able to investigate potential companies on your own, then a discount or online broker may fit the bill. Many individuals are finding that taking charge of their investments is an empowering experience. Once they become acquainted with all of the available information, many investors feel like they are in the best position to handle their investments and they are happy to be in the driver's seat.

Commissions charged by brokerage houses were deregulated in 1975, and this decision was truly the beginning of the ascent of the discount broker. Trades could be conducted for far less money than investors were used to paying at full-service brokerage firms like Merrill Lynch and Morgan Stanley Dean Witter. Discount brokers are now offering more services than ever before and, combined with all of the new and faster technology, investors have all of the investment information they need right at their disposal.

With the meteoric development and use of the Internet, the opportunity for self-education is virtually limitless. Beginning investors now have access to many of the same resources as full-service brokers. With this access to data, the demand for full-service brokers has been diminishing as the Internet continues to gain prominence. With a little enthusiasm and determination, you can find a wealth of information online that will keep you well-informed about everything from a company's new introductions to the 10 most highly traded stocks on any given day.

Some of the best Web sites were created by financial institutions, and investors have access to everything with just the click of a mouse—from real-time quotes to analyst reports to stock market basics. You can even communicate with other investors, who may offer you some great investment ideas. The proliferation of online discount brokers has made trading possible around-the-clock for a nominal fee. In some cases, you can make trades for under $10. Trading online is ideal if you have done your homework and know exactly which stock you want to own.

If you want someone else to do most of the legwork, then you might opt for a full-service broker. Of course, full-service brokers charge a premium for their input. There is no guarantee that a full-service broker will steer you in the direction of massive capital gains; however, you can get his or her input. If you want to work with a full-service broker, it's advisable to get a reference from someone you know and trust. Be on the lookout for brokers that engage in "churning."

If a broker is overly eager to buy and sell your stocks on a continual basis for no apparent reason, you may be the victim of churning. Churning is especially beneficial to brokers who work on commission—the more trades they make, the more pay they take home.

Find a broker who shares your basic investment philosophy and one who gives you several investment options to choose from. Feel free to request current company reports if you are unsure about which stocks would best suit your needs.

It's perfectly acceptable to ask your potential brokers questions pertaining to how long they have been in this business and about their formal education, their investment philosophy, and what sources they use to get the majority of their information. You may want to find out which investment publications they regularly read and which they find most helpful (and why). Find out if they rely only on their brokerage firm's reports when making stock recommendations. It may be in your best interest to work with a broker with a minimum of five years of investment experience because you want someone who has witnessed (and traded in) both bull and bear markets.

Becoming acquainted with the fee structure is crucial. In many cases, you may be charged for services that you didn't know you were getting—and wouldn't use even if you knew you could. You also want to inquire about the fees associated with ending, maintaining, and closing an account; getting checks; participating in investment profiles; buying and selling securities; and attending various seminars. To circumvent potential discrepancies, it's important that you obtain this information in writing and in advance—and not after the fact.

The National Association of Securities Dealers (NASD) can answer your questions about the practices of a particular broker by looking up his or her past record regarding any disciplinary actions taken or complaints registered against the broker. They can also confirm whether the broker is licensed to conduct business in your state of residence. You can reach them at 1-800-289-9999.

The NASD Regulation, Inc. is the independent subsidiary of the National Association of Securities Dealers charged with regulating the securities industry and the NASDAQ Stock Market. Through its many departments and offices, NASD Regulation's jurisdiction extends to more than 5,400 firms with more than 58,000 branch offices, and more than 505,000 securities industry professionals.

Another option is to utilize the services of financial planners. Such individuals go beyond handling just your investments—they can aid you in matters relating to insurance, taxes, trusts, and real estate. The cost of doing business with financial planners can range considerably. If you opt for a financial planner, it may be in your best interest to utilize the services of a fee-based planner in lieu of one that works solely on commission. If an individual works on commission alone, it may be in his or her best interest to encourage heavy trading in the investment options for which they get a commission. While some planners charge a flat hourly rate, other individuals may charge a fee that is based on your total assets and trading activity. In this type of arrangement, you are responsible to pay the financial planner even if you do not follow any of his or her suggestions. Other planners operate with a combination of fee-based charges and commission. Here, you may pay less per trade but you are also responsible for paying additional fees.

List of Online and Discount Brokers

Here is a listing of some of the numerous discount brokers available. Many offer you the opportunity to trade online, while most sport toll-free numbers for easy phone trading. Some online brokers are very popular with those who believe technology rules supreme (and that is a growing segment of the population). However, there are also many "hardliners" who are tired of faceless, nameless technology and want a toll-free number to speak to another human being if necessary. As fast as technology is, when something goes wrong, it's a painfully slow, complicated process to correct it. Most discount brokerage houses offer a choice between online trading AND toll-free numbers.

The following list contains just some of the many popular, easily accessible discount brokers throughout the United States. This list includes brokers with toll-free numbers, and most have online trading.

Accutrade. 1-800-228-3011.

Online trading at *www.accutrade.com*.

American Express Financial Direct. 1-800-658-4677.
Online trading at
www.americanexpress.com/direct.
Ameritrade. 1-800-669-3900.
Online trading at *www.ameritrade.com.*
Bull and Bear Securities. 1-800-262-5800.
No online trading thus far.
Charles Schwab and Co. 1-800-435-4500.
Online trading at *www.eschwab.com.*
High volume and low prices from one of the
biggest of the brokerage houses.
Datek Securities. 1-888-GODATEK.
Online trading at *www.datek.com.*
E*Trade. 1-800-786-2575.
Online trading at *www.etrade.com.*
High volume, very popular site with low prices.
Fleet Brokerage. 1-800-766-3000.
No online trading thus far.
Ichan and Company. 1-800-634-8518.
No online trading thus far.
Jack White and Company. 1-800-233-3411.
Online trading at *www.pawws.com/jwc.*
Marquette De Bary Company. 1-800-221-3305.
Online trading at *www.debary.com.*
Max Ule. 1-800-223-6642.
Online trading at *www.maxule.com.*
Quick and Reilly. 1-800-926-0600.
Online trading at *www.quick-reilly.com.*
Offering two online services for trading.
Tradex Brokerage Service. 1-800-522-3000.
No online trading thus far.

USAA Brokerage Services. 1-800-531-8343.
No online trading thus far.
Vanguard Discount Brokerage. 1-800-992-8372.
Online trading at *www.vanguard.com.*
The Wall Street Discount Corporation. 1-800-221-7870.
Online trading at *www.wsdc.com.*
Waterhouse Securities. 1-800-934-4410.
Online trading at *www.waterhouse.com.*
Your Discount Broker. 1-800-800-3215.
No online trading thus far.

Placing an Order (Buying and Selling)

When you're ready to place an order, either online or with a broker, you have several options: a market order, a limit order, a stop/limit order, or a stop/loss order. Any of these orders can be placed either for the day or GTC (good-till-canceled).

Market Order

When you want to buy or sell a stock at the current price, you can place a market order. This means that you want to buy or sell a certain stock at the price the stock is trading for when the order reaches the floor. In other words, you're buying or selling a given stock at the "going rate." Depending on whether you're buying or selling, the market price may differ. This is known as the bid or ask price, and the difference between these two prices is known as the spread. For example, Coca-Cola may have a bid price to sell at $65¼ per share and an asking price to buy at $65½ per share, making the spread one-quarter. Unlike Coca-Cola, securities that are thinly traded often have bigger spreads. For playing the role of the middleman, dealers in a security generally keep a large part of the spread. Middlemen are in the business of selling goods at a higher price than what they initially paid. Stock prices, especially in heavily traded stock, can change in just seconds. By the time your order is filled with a market order, you might find a slight difference in the price you were quoted.

Limit Order

Limit orders are placed if you don't want to purchase stock for more or sell a stock for less than a predetermined price. A limit order, along with other types of orders, can be placed as a day order or as a good-till-canceled (GTC) order. A day order is only good until the end of the trading day; a GTC order is good until it is canceled. Your order may not fill with either one of these two options; however, you have a greater chance of your order being filled with a GTC order since it can remain open for a longer period of time.

Buy

If you want to buy a stock for a specified price, you can place a limit order. If Cisco is currently trading at $105 and you want to buy 100 shares of Cisco if it dips to $100, you can place a limit order for 100 shares of Cisco at $100 per share. The order may fill for $100 per share if the price dips to that level. If it does not, your order will remain unfilled. Your order to buy stock may be filled for less than $100 per share if the stock hits $100 and trades at a lower price after it hits $100 per share. However, your order will not fill for more than $100.

Sell

If you own Cisco and want to sell the stock if it dips to $95 per share, you can place a limit order to sell. In this case, your order will fill for $95 per share. Your order to sell the stock may be filled for more than $95 per share if the stock hits $95 and trades at a higher price after it hits $95. However, your order will not fill for less than $95 per share.

Stop Order

Once your stock reaches a target figure in a stop order, it becomes a market order. Stop orders are a viable vehicle for investors who own a stock and are concerned about it falling too low.

Sell

If you purchase Disney at $40 per share, you could place a stop order for $30 to sell that stock if the price drops to $30. If the next trade after the stock reaches $30 is 29½ per share, you would sell your Disney stock for $29½ per share if your order is filled. The stop order turns into a market order as soon as the exchange price hits the predetermined figure. After the stock reaches $30 per share, it will be sold at the market price, which is the price of the next trade. This could be higher or lower than $30 per share.

Buy

You can also place a stop order to buy. If Disney is currently selling at $35 per share and you want to purchase the stock if it climbs to $40 because you think the price will continue to rise, it becomes a market order once it hits $40 per share. If the next trade after it reaches $40 per share is

$40½, you would buy your Disney stock for $40½ per share if your order is filled. After the stock reaches $40 per share, it will be bought at the market price, which is the price of the next trade. This could be higher or lower than $40½ per share.

Dividend Reinvestment Plans (DRIPs)

Dividend reinvestment plans offer shareholders a simple and inexpensive way to purchase stock directly through a company. This type of investment plan does not require the services of a broker. Such plans enable investors to purchase small amounts of common stock (in many cases, as little as $25) directly through the company. Depending on the company, there may be a small fee for handling your account, and you often need to have already purchased at least one share of the stock from a broker.

Dividend reinvestment plans may be a good choice for long-term investors who want to buy more shares of a certain stock on an ongoing basis. You can probably find a listing of companies that offer dividend reinvestment plans at your local library, or you can call a company directly to find out if they offer this service.

Investing in an Unpredictable World

If a company's future looks promising and its products and/or services are in great demand, stock prices will normally rise. Conversely, the price may dip if the company isn't living up to its expectations. Keep in mind that even if a company's earnings rose during a given quarter, the stock price might not go up (or it could drop) if Wall Street analysts were anticipating even greater earnings. Buying and selling of shares will affect the stock price, and rumors—among other factors—can influence the direction of a stock price. If there are no major problems within the company, this is usually an example of a short-term decline. Due to market fluctuations, the value of your stocks will often change on a daily basis. In many cases, a stock's price may tumble or escalate for no significant reason.

If you find that one of your stocks has taken a turn for the worse, you need to examine the reasons behind this downward activity. If it appears that the stock has been adversely affected for the short-term, a wise investor could take advantage of the situation by purchasing more stock rather than feeling like a victim. Companies with great product introductions, attractive profit margins, and a phenomenal growth rate will, ultimately, prevail.

On the other side of the coin, if you did not do your homework and the company does have serious, long-term problems, it's often best to cut your losses and rid yourself of the stock. Think of it as a learning experience. Even if you did thoroughly study a company, there may be other factors leading to its lower stock price that could not have been foreseen. The company may have had a turnover in its key management team, new competition may have entered the arena, or demand for its product or service may have diminished.

Although, for the most part, the market has been strong, it will inevitably take downturns and, in time, the odds are that it will rise back up again. The earlier in life you start investing, the longer you can keep your money in the market. Although past performance is no guarantee of future performance, history has shown that time is probably going to work in your favor when it comes to investing.

chapter five

Mutual Funds

What Is a Mutual Fund?

A mutual fund is an investment vehicle that pools the money of many investors and buys stocks, bonds, or other securities, depending on the type of fund. It is a way to utilize the skills of a professional money manager, who manages the fund and selects the specific investments that he or she feels will best lead the fund toward the goal the fund has set out to achieve. There are funds set up for a wide range of goals and financial plans. Funds can provide a steady flow of income or can be engineered for growth in the short or long term. The success of the fund depends on the sum of its parts, which are the individual stocks or bonds within the fund's portfolio.

Currently, the number of mutual funds is approaching eleven thousand. Consider that as recently as 1991 the number was just over three thousand and at the end of 1996 it was listed at around six thousand. Despite their recent surge in popularity, they are not new. The first fund, consisting of 45 stocks, was established in 1924.

Diversifying Your Portfolio with Mutual Funds

The risk of investing in a mutual fund is less than that of a single stock because the fund is managed professionally and because of diversification. Mutual funds offer you diversification without making you do all of the work. Funds can hold anywhere from a few select stocks to more than one hundred stocks, bonds, and money market instruments. While some funds own as few as 20 or 25 stocks, others like the Schwab1000 own one thousand stocks. The diversity minimizes much of your risk.

If, for example, you bought one stock on your own it could go either way. However, if you bought six stocks, it would be less likely that all six would go down. If three went down and three went up you would be even. If you saw two dropping, you could sell them and buy something else, while you were still earning money off the others. The mutual funds work on the same "safety in numbers" principle. Although there are funds with higher and lower risks, the comfort of many mutual funds is that they limit risk by balancing higher-risk investments with lower-risk/safer investments. Diversity acts to your advantage as it protects you against greater swings in the market, be it the stock or bond market.

One of the reasons mutual funds can diversify so successfully is that when you invest in a mutual fund you are pooling your money with other investors. Having a larger group of investors allows the fund much greater buying power. It also allows you as the investor to stretch your money much farther. Some funds allow you to invest as little as $500, which then gets divided up into the various ownings of the mutual fund. Your $500 is now investing in perhaps fifty stocks and ten bonds. You could not have done this by purchasing stocks and bonds individually—the individual commissions alone would have eaten up your money.

Further diversification can also come from buying more than one fund. You can also allocate your assets into different types of funds. If you buy into a few funds in different categories, you'll have that much more diversification and that much less technical risk. (It's usually not advisable to have more than six or seven mutual funds at a given time or you can start to counterbalance your efforts to construct a strong portfolio.) Your portfolio might include, for example:

A more conservative bond fund
A "tech" fund to cash in on a hot industry
A more high-risk international fund
A low-risk, blue-chip fund
A growth fund

But beware that the more aggressive the fund (the more risky), the more volatile the fund will be. There are several reasons a fund may be volatile: fluctuations in the stock market; changing interest rates (particularly pertaining to bonds); foreign currency rates; and fund management. Also, a fund that is actively buying and selling more heavily will often be more volatile. Look to see if similar funds, in the same category, are also experiencing similar volatility. If, however, your fund is acting differently from similar funds, look more closely at the management and what direction the mutual fund is taking.

Short-term volatility is not at all uncommon for mutual funds. While you can lose money, the odds are strongly in your favor that the fund will bounce back if you hold onto it over time, particularly if it is a domestic-based stock (equity) fund.

Stock (Equity) Funds

The hottest and most talked about mutual funds on the market are the equity, or stock, funds. These are primarily made up of individual stocks purchased (at least 75 or 80 percent) by the fund. Your potential profit is the result of having a fund manager who has accumulated more winners than losers in the funds and more shares of the winners. The stocks comprising the fund are most often common stocks, and the fund managers purchase them based on potential earnings of companies, while looking at the issuer's management, track record, and financial condition. They also look at how the company fares in the overall industry in which it sits. In other words, in an industry such as health, they are looking to see if a company is one of the leaders in its field or lagging behind its competitors.

Following are some of the many types of stock funds.

Growth Funds

A growth fund is less concerned with the current price of a stock and more concerned that the sales and earnings of the company will grow (then the resulting stock will rise). The idea is not the traditional "buy low, sell high," but buy at whatever price and watch the company build momentum, get on a roll, and grow. Growth investors seek out companies that have tremendous potential based perhaps on new products or services not being offered elsewhere or excellent management. In recent years growth funds have outperformed value funds, but that has not been the case in the past. Long-term growth funds look to capitalize on larger, steadily growing companies like Microsoft, while aggressive growth funds involve smaller companies that are taking off fast, like Internet start-ups.

Aggressive Growth Funds

These are the funds that generate the most press, because when they are going well they are going very well. Some of these have, of late, produced tremendous results. For example, the UltraOTC Pro Fund saw a return of 185.3 percent in 1998. Aggressive growth funds look for companies poised to grow in the short term, which is why they are riskier investments. You'll find many of the recent aggressive growth funds on the NASDAQ.

Growth and Income Funds

You might also choose to go with a fund that specifically seeks out companies that not only are expected to grow but also companies that will pay dividends. Such a fund provides steady income, which is attractive to anyone who likes to maintain cash flow even during major dips in the market. A growth and income fund can also work very well for an individual who may be retiring but still wants to have money in the market. Such a fund will provide cash toward living expenses while allowing the investor to maintain some capital. There are also straight income funds, which are more conservative by nature, seeking as their primary objective to pay you dividends from consistently well-performing (usually major) companies. One of the nicest aspects of an income fund is that the companies that pay dividends, hence those in the portfolio, are usually not affected greatly by downturns in the market.

Value Funds

A value mutual fund invests in stocks that are undervalued. These are companies that—for one reason or another—are struggling, and the stock prices are low while the actual value of the company may be much higher. Sometimes it's a matter of too much market competition; in other cases it's a company that is lagging behind in the latest technology or has not done anything of major impact of late. However, if the P/E ratio and book value of the stocks in the portfolio are good, the fund can be worthwhile. Value investors are saying that if a company is worth $40 per share and they can buy it at $20 per share, they want to take the stock at that lower (value) price. Although in recent years value funds have been outperformed by growth funds, they adhere to the old adage "buy low, sell high."

Sector Funds

Sector funds diversify, but only in one sector. Rather than spread your investment around between various types of industries, they choose stocks pertaining to one particular industry, such as oil, health, utilities, or technology stocks. Tech stocks in recent years would have been an excellent choice for a sector fund as some have seen huge returns. Certain industries, such as utilities or companies in the food industry, will be less volatile and more consistent than others that are more cyclical. The idea behind buying a sector fund is often, not unlike market timing, selecting an industry that you foresee taking off in the next few years. For example, the new health-related technology has people looking at stocks pertaining to companies that are doing new and innovative things in the medical area. Internet sector funds may also generate more attention, but be careful that an overabundance of Internet providers doesn't bring prices back down to earth. A sector fund can give you a bumpy ride if you are planning to be there for the long haul. Often such a fund works best as part of a larger portfolio that diversifies across industries and sectors.

International and Global Funds

Many international funds spread your investment around, buying into markets worldwide, while others look at the economic potential of one country. International specialized funds have not fared well over the past three or even five years. This doesn't mean there are not some winners, primarily being the European funds in recent years. Overall, however, the big gains have not been in this area of late.

Usually not the place for a beginning investor, these can be risky funds because of the high volatility of many overseas markets. Besides, other funds may already be investing a small portion into overseas investments, thus dabbling in the arena and letting you have some foreign diversification.

Index Funds

From 1987 through 1997 the S&P 500 Index performed better than 81 percent of the general equity funds, even if many have claimed otherwise. (After all, 81 percent of the people on Wall Street, including pretzel vendors, will claim they can beat the S&P).

While Index funds seem like an easy way out, they are also an easy way to stick with a successful benchmark that everyone uses. They allow you to be in various sectors and to invest in both growth and value stocks, giving you maximum diversification. Index funds will have lower costs since there are not a lot of transactions and there are no management decisions to be made.

Balanced Funds

Balanced funds derive capital gains from a mixed bag of investments primarily consisting of stocks and bonds. This is ideal for those investors who do not want to allocate their own portfolios. Balanced funds provide maximum diversity and allow their managers to balance more volatile investments with safer, low-risk investments such as bonds. They are usually designed for the more-conservative investor who does not want to go too heavily into equities. Naturally, since this fund can have a wide range of investments, it is important to look over the fund's portfolio and get an idea of what makes up the "balance" in your balanced fund. The combination of good returns (category average of 13.1 percent for 10-year returns from 1988 through 1998) plus nice yields make these funds worthy of your attention.

Socially Responsible Funds

"Socially responsible" depends largely on the fund manager's definition of social responsibility. Some funds steer clear of products that use animal testing; many do not invest in companies involved with the defense industry, guns, or tobacco; others concern themselves with child labor issues. Some funds use all of the above or other criteria. Dreyfus Third Century Fund and PAX World are two of the most successful, best-known funds in this area. They are looking for protection of the environment and natural resources, occupational health and safety, life supportive goods and services, and companies that do not sell liquor, firearms, or tobacco products. The intentions are good and the funds are profitable.

Large-Cap, Mid-Cap, and Small-Cap Funds

Investing in different types of cap funds primarily serves to diversify your investments. You don't want all of the same sized companies because their success does go in cycles. In 1998, large-cap funds sitting with Coca-Cola, General Electric, IBM, and other giant companies performed better than the small-cap mutual funds. One of the possible reasons is the tremendous growth in investing to a much wider sector of the population. No longer are the Wall Street insiders the only ones seeking out stocks and funds. As more and more people get into the stock market and buy into funds from their home PCs, they may be comfortable buying the larger companies with which they are familiar. Some small-cap companies, such as those in the technical sector, are also very well-known to a very literate computer population, which is why a company like Intel or Dell Computer can also shine. As the newer online investors become more savvy, they too will branch out from safer, more familiar territory and explore the many growing companies.

Asset Allocation Fund

Not unlike a balanced fund, an asset allocation fund maximizes diversification. The fund is managed to encompass a broad range of investment vehicles and asset classes. If managed correctly, an asset allocation fund will center around a mix of stocks, bonds, and short-term instruments and distribute the percentage of holdings in each area according to which is providing better returns. Whereas a balanced fund tries to maintain a balance between stocks and bonds, an asset allocation fund (depending on market conditions) can be 75 percent stocks one year and (should the economy be experiencing a bear market) 75 percent bonds the next year. Factoring in each type of investment, the fund manager has a wide range of choices across asset groups, and is not locked into a set percentage allocated to one type of investment.

Closed-End Mutual Funds

As opposed to being another category of fund, closed-end funds are a broader grouping of mutual funds that include several fund categories that you can buy into. They are unique, however, in several respects.

While most mutual funds are open-end, meaning they will continue offering shares as long as they have buyers, closed-end mutual funds have a fixed amount of shares that they can sell to investors. A closed-end fund, or CEF, is publicly traded. An initial public offering (IPO), like the offering to introduce a new stock to the public, is where the CEF begins. The shares then trade like stocks on the American or New York Stock Exchange.

Closed-end funds differ from their open-end counterparts in that by selling a specific number of shares they do not keep growing indefinitely as more investors put money into the fund. Like open-end funds, they have a fund manager who buys and sells stocks, but they remain within the structure and limits of the fund dictated by how many shares there are to sell and at what price.

Another distinct feature of closed-end funds is that, unlike an open-end fund where you buy or sell your shares with the fund directly, with a CEF you buy and sell shares with other investors. If there is a greater demand for the shares, the market price will rise and you will make a profit. This is called a premium. The market price, less the NAV, will give you your premium earned. You can also sell a CEF at a lower price. In this regard, the buying and selling of CEFs is similar to that of the bond market.

Since closed-end funds require you either to know when there is an initial public offering or to have a seller from which you can buy, they are bought through brokerage houses, meaning there will be a commission. There are brokers who specialize in closed-end mutual funds.

Finding a Mutual Fund That's Right for You

To choose your mutual fund, it's a matter of matching your goals, risk level, time frame, and the amount of money you have to invest with the fund category that suits your needs and comfort level. Even if you know you could be investing in a high-risk aggressive growth fund, you may find yourself staying up worrying at night if you do so. What's right for you is what you believe will help you reach your goals and, from doing your homework, what you believe the future holds.

As for selecting a fund family, it is often suggested that you look for one that has been around a while, unless you're going with an emerging industry such as tech stocks, where the newer fund families may all have been around for about the same length of time. The more-established fund families can show you 10-year returns, which you can compare against comparable funds in other fund families that have been around a while. They can also give you an indication of how the fund has fared during the bear markets and how long it took them to recover. Naturally some of this will depend on the fund manager, but you have a better chance of finding a fund manager with 10 years' experience at the helm of a fund at an older, more-established company. Look at the 10-year returns and see if the same fund manager was there over that time period. If you look at 10-year returns and see that the current manager has only been on board for three years, those 10-year returns won't mean as much.

Judging past performance of a fund can be more tricky than it might seem by glancing at five- and 10-year returns. Sectors or industries that are in vogue during one period may not be during the next. For example, if technology stocks returns were to drop to a modest return over the next three years, looking back in five years at their 10- and even five-year total returns is going to show a distorted picture because of how well they are doing now. One spectacular year of 90 percent growth, followed by four years of 10 percent growth, is still going to average 26 percent growth per year, which would not be a good indicator of how that fund is performing at the end of year five, when you are looking to buy it. Also, a sector that has not fared well over a stretch of time may be on the upswing due to new products, consumer needs, or public awareness (as with the socially responsible stocks). This won't show up in past performance. The same holds true for the large- and small-cap companies. A fund that invests in small companies will not see large returns when the trend leans toward the large corporations, as it has done in the late 1990s. But if that trend is about to change in 2001, it is not reflected. The best you can do is look at each measure of past performance, read up on future expectations, and try to make an informed decision. Remember—long-term five- and 10-year returns are important, but they are only part of the larger picture.

Before you make your selection, you should also check out the fund manager, understand the load (or no-load) and costs, evaluate the other fees and expenses, and above all, get and read the prospectus for each fund you are considering—all of which are detailed below. Once you finally make a decision, expect to be in the fund for at least one year, and usually five or more. Mutual funds are not generally thought of as a short-term investment.

Fund Managers

To assess a good fund manager, you need to look at his or her background over several years. You want to look for consistency in management of the fund or previous funds. You also want to see that the fund manager is holding true to his or her fund's financial goals.

You should also look closely at a mutual fund's portfolio. While you may not be familiar with each and every purchase, you can ascertain whether they are following the latest trends or bucking the system. If you have heard, for example, that a certain market, such as automobiles, is taking a downturn, and the fund manager is buying heavily in that area, it will mean one of two things: either he or she is buying now for an anticipated turnaround (value investing), or he or she is not keeping up with the market's news.

You should also look at how the fund manager fared during the down markets of 1990 and 1997. See how quickly their funds rebounded. Did he or she panic and make drastic moves or hold on tight and ride out the storm? Naturally it will depend on the type of fund and the particular holdings. The manager's response is worth taking note of, since the market does go through volatile periods.

You also need to check out a new fund manager if you own a fund and the manager changes. A new fund manager needs to show that he or she can work within the structure of the particular fund, holding true to the goal of that fund. Fund size and assets can matter as well. A manager who has handled a $2 billion fund successfully may not be as comfortable when handed a $20 billion figure in a larger fund. Some managers are only successful with a finite amount of funds. You might also want to know whether or not this fund manager is working closely with a team of analysts or doing it all on his or her own. If the latter is the case, you could be in trouble when the manager moves to another fund and takes along his or her secrets.

Forbes, *Kiplingers*, *Money*, *Morningstar*, and other sources will rate the mutual funds and often give you the "lowdown" or profile on the fund manager.

Loads, No Loads, and Operating Costs

A loaded fund means you are paying a commission to someone who has helped you determine which fund to purchase. A no-load fund means you have bought the fund on your own, usually through a toll-free number. The choice is yours depending on how much help, guidance, or hand holding you are seeking when buying mutual funds. The investor who does his or her homework and knows which fund is designed to meet his or her goals and needs can simply dial the fund and buy it without paying an additional commission. However, if searching for the right fund is taking hours out of your potential income-earning time, or time spent on the pursuit of enjoying your life, you may be better paying a commission with a load fund and utilizing your time in other ways.

While no-loads have gained an edge on loaded funds, many companies have started offering loaded no-loads. Naturally these loaded no-loads have catches to them whereby you will be paying a fee somewhere down the line for the privilege of not paying a fee. Whether the costs are for some types of "special benefits," a personal finance report, or some other accompanying service, the bottom line is that these are not commission-free funds. In short, "no-loads" by any other name are essentially loaded funds. Therefore, it's to your advantage as a new investor to buy either basic loads or no-loads. AND, when buying loaded funds, make sure you are told of each fee that can be charged; you deserve no surprises if the fund family wants your business.

Operating costs are also part of mutual funds. This is the money spent to keep the fund afloat. Along with administrative expenses, the analysts and fund manager also need to get paid advisory fees for their hard work investing your money. Expense ratios range from less than .25 percent to more than 2.5 percent. It is important to take note of the operating costs to determine how much of a bite they are taking out of your profits.

Fees and Expenses

Generally listed as the "expense ratio" are several costs that shareholders will pay for services and management of the fund. While the Securities and Exchange Commission is closely monitoring funds to make sure that shareholders are aware of all the expenses related to their fund, it's important that you as an investor understand the basics behind these fees and have a sense of what to look for on your own. International funds often have higher expense ratios than domestic funds because they are dealing with companies overseas.

A mutual fund operates like a smaller business within the structure of the larger fund family. It is an entity unto itself in that the fund does not interact with other funds under the same umbrella company. They share printed materials and costs, such as advertising the financial group, but from the perspective of the fund family, each fund is handled separately. In other words, the expense ratio you're paying for "Fund A" will not spill over to pay the manager of "Fund B."

Fees generally include the following:

Service fees. These fees are used for financial compensation of the planners, analysts, and brokers who assist customers with fund-related questions and provide information and advice regarding the fund. Accounting and legal services may also be included.

Administrative fees. These are the fees associated with office staff, office space, and other fundamentals to running a business, including equipment. Sometimes these funds are absorbed under management fees. Office expenses incurred by a fund also include online support and information, check processing, auditing, record keeping, shareholders' reports, and printed matter.

Management fees. This is the percentage that goes to the fund manager. This can be a flat percentage or one set up to coincide with the growth of the fund based on returns. The bigger the fund gets, in terms of assets, the lower the percentage will generally be.

12b-1 fee. This is a fee used primarily for marketing or advertising the fund. Since there are so many mutual funds on the market, it is becoming increasingly important for fund families to advertise. Your fee is not just a contribution to the fund's advertising budget but will hopefully help the fund to grow—and as the fund grows, there will be more money available. Therefore, the fund will have greater leverage to buy more holdings, which can—with a good fund manager—be to your advantage. In fact, some funds report that because of advertising, their overall expense ratios have gone down as the funds have grown. So for those who do not like the 12b-1 fee, remember that it can work in your favor.

Other Costs

One other "cost," which isn't related to the fund directly but to the government, is an old standard: taxes. On the plus side, if you lose money on the fund you won't be paying capital gains tax, but that's hardly a reason to celebrate. If you see a profit, you will pay taxes on dividends or on capital gains distributions paid to you while owning shares of the fund, or on your profits (capital gains) from selling your shares of the fund. You may also be subject to state taxes, depending on the state in which you reside.

You may also see capital gains based on the trading done by the fund manager, even though you haven't sold any of your shares. These can hit you for taxes. Buying funds late in the year is ill-advised because you can be hit for higher taxes as the fund is just about to distribute their capital gains.

The Prospectus: The Mutual Fund Bible

In a highly competitive fund market, some funds are actually trying to soften the legalese in which the fund's prospectus is written. However, some are still very hard to decipher. The problem is that while the important information is in there somewhere, it can be hard to find in the midst of a wealth of legal jargon. Therefore, it's to your advantage to read the prospectus with an eye for specific areas of importance.

A few of the important details you should review include:

The fund's objective. The fund should have a clear statement of what the objective is. Is it aggressive growth? Current income? If the objective is unclear, the mutual fund manager has more leeway. It also means your intentions for choosing that particular fund may not be carried out. If the fund objective is not clear, either seek out a fund that is more clearly defined, ask someone in the fund's investment information department, or follow the old rule of thumb: do your homework. Look up the fund's current holdings.

The investment risks. The mutual fund prospectus should discuss the level of risks the fund will take in conjunction with their objective. Stock funds should discuss the types of stocks they are buying. Look at the warnings they're giving you. Are they telling you about the currency and political risks involved with their international holdings?

Investment breakdown. The fund should clearly lay out the percentage of holdings they are committed to in each fund group. They should say, for example, that the management is required to hold at least 70 percent in U.S. bonds, or 80 percent in common stocks, or no more than 20 percent in international investments. The breakdown and parameters of the fund give you an idea where your money will be invested.

Costs and fees. A fee table should outline all the fees associated with that fund. Read them carefully and make sure you are left with no surprises. Operating costs, loads, and any other fees should all be included.

Financial history. A prospectus will also give you the history of that mutual fund. The financial information should provide the per-share results for the life of the fund—or for funds that have been around for a long time, at least the past 10-year history. You can gauge the total return of the fund on an annual basis. You can also look at the year-end net asset values, the fund's expense ratio, and any other information that will help you gauge how the fund has performed over time. You can check on dividend payments, if it is an income fund, or see the types of holdings the fund has sold and purchased.

In the end, the prospectus should answer all of your questions and concerns about a particular fund. Obtaining a prospectus, by the way, should be as easy as calling the fund's toll-free number.

Buying and Selling Mutual Funds

So, you're ready to buy a mutual fund. The first thing you need to know is how the price is set. The net asset value (NAV) of the fund is the first price you need to be aware of. It is essentially calculated by taking the net asset of the fund and dividing that by the number of outstanding shares. Therefore, if you had a fund with $1 million in net assets and 105,000 outstanding shares, the NAV would be 9.52. That gives you a number by which to gauge the fund, based on everything the fund owns minus its liabilities.

The price at which you can buy shares of the fund, the public offering price (POP), can be the same or higher depending on whether there is a load or not on the fund. A no-load fund will not have a higher POP, while a loaded fund might see the same 9.52 listed at 9.77 to include the load.

At this point you are buying shares in a similar manner to how you buy shares of individual stocks. Therefore, if you wanted 300 shares of this no-load fund at 9.52 per share it would cost you $2,856. Often funds are bought in round numbers for the sake of easier bookkeeping on your part, meaning you might enter a fund with a minimum purchase of $5,000 (some are higher and many are lower). Therefore, you would invest $5,000 and have 525 shares ($5,000 divided by 9.52). The loaded fund would simply either cost you more per share, or if you bought $5,000 worth, you would have to deduct the .25 load, giving you slightly fewer shares.

Where to Purchase Mutual Funds

Funds today are as easy to purchase as making a phone call or a trip to your computer. Fund families (large investment firms or brokerage houses with many funds), seeing the surge in popularity and wanting to make funds easily accessible to all investors, have toll-free numbers and Web sites that make it easy for you to buy and sell mutual funds. Transactions are also, occasionally, made by the old fashioned method of "snail" mail.

Electronic trading has allowed investors to trade at all hours from the comfort of their own homes. It's not hard to find the Top 10, Top 20, or Top 50 funds on your browser, as rated by some leading financial source, and then buy them online.

For those who need to put their hands on their money in a hurry and convert mutual fund shares to cash, another benefit of mutual funds is liquidity. A phone call allows you to sell your shares in the fund at its current Net Asset Value (NAV, or posted rate per share), and you should have your money in three or four business days.

Mutual Fund Families

There are numerous mutual fund families to choose from (Dreyfus, Fidelity, Schwab, etc.). They are essentially brokerage houses. They serve as an umbrella for a number of funds, and they offer various other financial services. Depending on the financial institution the mutual fund selection can be very large; fund families generally offer a wide variety of funds in each broad category to match differing goals. One advantage to staying within a particular fund family is that it is easier to switch funds, and there is not usually an associated cost or fee.

Following are just some of the numerous fund families, based on overall size. This does not mean that a small fund family with five funds may not have three of the most successful funds of the year. Some small fund companies have some hugely successful funds. We simply couldn't list them all.

Advantus	1-800-665-6005
Aim	1-800-347-4246
Alliance	1-800-227-4618
American Century	1-800-345-2021
American Funds	1-800-421-4120
BlackRock	1-800-441-7762
Delaware Investments	1-800-523-4640
Dreyfus	1-800-373-9387
Eaton Vance	1-800-225-6265
Evergreen	1-800-343-2898
Federated	1-800-341-7400
Fidelity	1-800-544-8888
Franklin	1-800-342-5236

Hancock	1-800-225-5291
IDS	1-800-437-3133
Invesco	1-800-525-8085
Kemper	1-800-621-1048
Merrill Lynch	1-800-637-3863
MFS	1-800-637-2929
Morgan Stanley Dean Witter	1-800-869-6397
Oppenheimer	1-800-525-7048
PBHG	1-800-433-0051
Phoenix	1-800-243-4361
Pioneer	1-800-225-6292
Prudential	1-800-225-1852
Putnam	1-800-225-1581
Schwab	1-800-435-4000
Scudder	1-800-225-2470
Smith Barney	1-800-451-2010
Stagecoach	1-800-222-8222
Strong	1-800-368-1030
Templeton	1-800-292-9293
T. Rowe Price	1-800-638-5660
USAA	1-800-382-8722
Vanguard	1-800-851-4999
Van Kempen	1-800-341-2911

Strategies

You can use similar strategies with mutual funds as you do when playing the market and buying individual stocks. One strategy that can work well with mutual funds is dollar-cost averaging. Essentially, this is where you invest a fixed sum of money into the mutual fund on a regular basis regardless of where the market stands. Retirement plans and 401(k) plans are generally built on this principle, except they have restrictions on the withdrawal end. Following a regular investment schedule, whether it's weekly, monthly, or bimonthly, you are not trying to time the stocks in the fund's portfolio. Frequently an investor will decide to have the same amount of money automatically withdrawn from his or her account and invested into the mutual fund on a consistent weekly, or monthly, basis—not unlike a 401(k) or retirement plan. Over time, a fixed amount invested regularly, as opposed to buying a fixed number of shares, will reduce your average cost per share over time. In essence you are buying more shares when the prices are low and fewer shares when the prices are high.

Dollar-cost averaging also eliminates the popular "timing the market" game played by the professionals—sometimes for better and sometimes for worse. Market timing is essentially trying to determine the peaks and valleys of the market and buy and sell accordingly. This is usually not advised for beginning investors. The part of dollar-cost averaging that can be difficult emotionally is that by investing on a regular basis you will also be investing during bear markets. Direct deposit makes this a little easier. It's also easier with mutual funds, where you know that a good fund manager should be setting up the portfolio with stocks that will best recover from a market downturn, rather than with one stock, which could take a longer time to rebound.

Keeping Track

Financial publications, national newspapers, and local newspapers are all places to keep tabs on your mutual funds. Add to that the Financial News Network and online services, and it's likely that you can find all the important information on your mutual fund on a daily basis.

First and foremost, make sure you know EXACTLY what symbol your fund goes by and don't forget the letter following the fund, being the A, B, C, D issue. The letters primarily refer to the type of load, front load, back load, no load, etc. It's amazing how many people have realized, after several days or weeks, that they either can't find their fund or have been following the wrong fund.

Once you have found your fund, you need to understand the letters and numbers that make up the mutual fund listings. Among the many symbols and numbers you will see included the name of the fund family, the name of the specific fund, and the fund's objective (OBJ), which will be listed such as CV (convertible fund), LG (large-cap growth), or GL (government, long-term bond fund).

The NAV (Net Asset Value) is the current price per share of the fund, or the price at which the fund is selling shares. By multiplying the number of shares you own by that price per share you can tell the current value of your fund. By comparing this to the total at which you bought the mutual fund, you will know how your fund is doing.

Next, the listing will have changes, or the movement of the fund, by either the day, week, or YTD percent (which is year-to-date total percentage, including reinvested dividends and capital gains). All of this will give you an idea of which direction the fund is going.

Some listings will include "Down Market" or "Bear Market," which will indicate how the fund has performed during the downturns in the market. Again, this is information you'll want when looking to purchase a fund.

A volatility ranking will tell you how much of a roller-coaster ride you can expect. Such a rating is the "beta" of the mutual fund. This is not generally found in daily listings but on comparison listings of funds over time. This can ease your mind on a day-to-day basis—you see sudden drops and then realize that this fund will have its share of peaks and valleys on route to (hopefully) showing solid gains.

chapter six

Bonds and Bond Funds

Bond Basics

Bonds are essentially a loan to a company, municipality, or the government (or a foreign government) of money to be paid back at a set date in the future. For lending them the money, the borrower (or issuer of the bond) agrees to pay you a rate of interest. Bonds are sold in specific increments and can be bought on a short-term basis (up to five years), intermediate-term basis (generally seven to 10 years), or a long-term basis (usually around 20 to 30 years). Longer-term bonds will pay higher yields (they've averaged higher than six percent over the last 50 years) than short-term bonds. They will, over the time you hold them, fluctuate more with changes in interest rates, which primarily matters to you if you are trying to sell a bond.

A bond will have a date of final maturity, which is the date at which the bond will return your principal, or initial investment. Some types of bonds can be "called" earlier, which means that the lender pays you back at an earlier date. A $5,000 bond is therefore worth $5,000 upon maturity as long as the issuer does not default on the payment. The interest you receive while holding the bond is your "perk," so to speak, for lending the money. Interest is usually paid semi-annually or annually, and it compounds at different rates.

Bonds can be bought directly as new issues from the government, from a municipality, or from a company. Bonds can also be bought from bond traders, brokers, or dealers (as they're called) on the secondary market. The bond market will dictate how easily you can buy or sell and at what price. Savings bonds can also be purchased through some banks.

As a bondholder, unlike a stockholder, you are not taking part in the success or failure of the company. Shares of stock will rise and fall in conjunction with how the company is doing. In the case of bonds, you will receive interest on your loan (from the bond issuer) and get your principal back at the date of maturity, regardless of how well a company is doing—unless, of course, they go bankrupt. Bonds are therefore referred to as "fixed income" investments because you know how much you will get back unless you sell, and then the price will need to be determined based on the market.

Bond Ratings

Corporate bonds and some municipal bonds are rated by financial analysts at Standard & Poor's (S&P) and Moody's, among others. They are rated to give you an idea of how sound the issuer of the bond actually is as a company, municipality, or corporation.

A high rating, or grade, of AAA (S&P) or Aaa (Moody's) is the highest quality bond. This means you are dealing with a sound financial corporation or municipality. Generally bonds of AAA, AA, A, or BBB (Aaa, Aa, A, or Bbb in Moody's system) are considered high-quality bonds. BB or B bonds are more questionable, because the companies are lacking some of the characteristics of the top-level corporations. Anything below B, such as C- or D-level bonds, are considered low-grade or "junk" bonds. Obviously they are investments in companies that have a much greater chance of defaulting on the bond. These companies, however, may also be new emerging entities that at some point in time may be the next Disney. If you pick the right rising company, a "junk" or high-yield bond can be very successful. BUT the risks are high.

Types of Bonds

Zero Coupon Bonds

Zero coupon bonds can be issued by companies, government agencies, or municipalities. Known as "zeros," these bonds do not pay interest periodically as most bonds do. Instead they are purchased at a discount and pay you a higher rate (both interest and principal) when they reach maturity. In other words, it's like lending someone $100 and having them tell you that they'll give you an extra $50 on a specific date when they pay you back, but they will give you nothing in between.

Corporate Bonds

Buying corporate bonds (or "corporates" as they're also known) means you are lending the company some money for a specified amount of time and at a specific rate of interest. While corporate bonds are more risky than government or municipal bonds, long-term corporate bonds, over the past 50 years, have outperformed their government and municipal counterparts. Unlike the United States government, however, companies can—and do—go bankrupt, which can turn your well-intentioned bond certificates into wallpaper.

Corporates are generally issued in multiples of either $1,000 or $5,000, and you are paid interest annually or semi-annually. Corporate bonds pay higher yields at maturity than various other bonds (of course, the income you receive is taxable at both the federal and state level).

There are different types of corporate bonds to choose from. Debentures are unsecured bonds backed only by the company's general credit. This is the heading that most corporate bonds fall under. Guaranteed bonds are backed by a larger or parent company that will cover the principal if the bond from its subsidiary company is not able to pay. Collateral trust bonds are backed by collateral from the issuing company. Mortgage bonds are types of collateral bonds that are backed by real estate or similar property.

Convertible bonds can be converted into shares of stock in the company in which you purchased the bond. Essentially the company is saying that instead of paying you by check or in money at the maturity of the bond, it pays you by converting your bonds to shares of stock. If you are looking at a convertible bond, look at how the stock of the company is doing. For the most part, convertible bonds are somewhere between stocks and bonds in the wide world of risk. People often avoid them because they can be confusing.

United States Government Bonds

Backed by the full faith and credit of the U.S. government, these bonds are as safe as any investment you can find. Government bonds can be purchased directly from the Treasury Department, with no broker's fee (The Bureau of the Public Debt, Division of Customer Services, Washington, DC 20239, 202-874-4000). Many investors do not bother looking for government bond funds but simply purchase their own government investment vehicles since it is so easy to do.

The Name Is Bond, U.S. Savings Bond

There are different types of U.S. savings bonds to choose from. You can obtain EE, HH, or the new I Bonds. There are other bonds still in circulation, such as the H bonds, which were issued up until 1979.

The new I bonds are the first new government bonds issued in nearly 20 years. Similar to the EE Bonds, the I is called an accrual bond, which means the interest is always added (not paid out to the bond owner) to the value of the bond. These bonds are purchased at face value, or original maturity, and have a total life of 30 years, at which point they will no longer pay interest. The interest rate is made up of two parts. The first part is a fixed rate, which is assigned when you buy it and stays with the bond for the life of the bond. The second part is an inflation-adjusted portion, which is tied to the consumer price index (which goes up or down every six months). That is added to the fixed rate every six months. The variable part of the bond is tied to inflation, hence the I name.

I bonds can be purchased in denominations of either $50, $100, $200, $500, $1,000, $5,000, or $10,000. You need to hold onto an I bond for at least six months before redeeming it. After that you can cash it at any financial institution that handles bonds. However, if you cash it before five years, you will lose three months of interest.

Treasury Bonds

Treasury bonds are issued in denominations of anywhere from $1,000 on up. Every six months you will receive interest and you can, if you so choose, through Treasury Direct, have the interest from your bond deposited directly into your bank account or money market fund. They are, like U.S. savings bonds, as safe an investment as you'll find and are backed by the full faith and credit of the U.S. government.

You can buy treasury bonds directly from the Federal Reserve Bank or from the Bureau of Public Debt. Quarterly auctions are held, and you can put in a noncompetitive bid, meaning you will get the bond at whatever the current rate is. You can also buy through a brokerage house, but you will pay a commission.

Beyond purchasing from the government, you can buy or sell treasury bonds on the bond market (which you can't do with savings bonds). Like other bonds, it's a matter of buying and/or selling at the right market price, which varies based on economic factors. The market for treasury bonds is enormous, so there's always a buyer or seller, but not necessarily at the price you want.

Treasury bonds are not callable, and you can have them for a long time, such as 30 years. If you already own bonds and locked in a good rate before the current rates dropped, you have been enjoying better returns than anything you will get today. Rates on long-term treasury bonds have been in the 5 percent to 6 percent range of late. With inflation low, it's not a bad investment, especially since you do not pay federal or state taxes on the interest income. This makes your yield equal to that of slightly higher-yield investments where you are paying taxes, especially in states with high state taxes.

Municipal Bonds

Munis, as they're called, are very popular for their tax-free advantages. States, cities, towns, municipalities, and government entities issue them. The yields on municipal bonds generally won't pay as high as those of their corporate counterparts. However, when you consider the yield after the taxes are paid from the corporate bond, the munis often don't look too bad, particularly in a state with high state taxes. You need to report tax-exempt interest on tax returns, but it is just for record-keeping purposes.

Tax-exempt municipal bonds make sense most of the time. However, if you have a tax-exempt retirement plan, which includes IRAs, you should not be looking to include such bonds since you are already not being taxed in the plan.

Municipal bonds will cost you $5,000 or a multiple of $5,000, or you can look for a municipal bond fund that will require less money to invest in. Yields will vary, like other bonds, based on the interest rates. Actual prices for traded bonds will be listed in the financial pages. Prices will vary based on the size of the order of bonds traded and the market. Like other bonds, you can sell a muni on the secondary market and, depending on the current rate, receive a higher rate of return than that at which you bought the bond.

Municipal bond funds can be national, investing in municipalities nationwide; statewide, investing in specific state municipalities; or local, investing in local municipalities. If you are in a state with high taxes you may find these funds to be appealing because you avoid such taxes. You may be taxed if you buy a municipal bond from another state.

Bond Mutual Funds

Like stock funds, bond funds buy bonds in bulk quantity. They are also categorized into different bond groupings depending on the types of bonds they buy. One of the nicest features about a bond fund is liquidity. When you purchase a single bond, your money is tied into the bond until maturity. You can sell the bond, but sometimes bonds can be more difficult to sell because they trade in the bond market. In a bond fund, buying and selling the bonds is the job of the fund manager, which takes many of the complications associated with understanding bonds away from you.

For someone seeking income from a mutual fund, a bond fund, thanks to interest, can provide a monthly check. Such a dividend can be especially welcome to someone who is retiring, or simply as income support. It is comforting to get a steady income when the stock or bond market is down. If you are not looking for a dividend check, the money can be reinvested into the fund. Since a bond fund is buying as many as hundreds of bonds with all different dates of maturity, there is always a bond paying a dividend and very often one coming due and being reinvested. Like stock funds, the diversification is something you could not accomplish on your own without a great deal of money and a lot of research—not to mention that individually you would pay more to buy each individual bond, whereas in a fund you are saving money and only paying the operating fees and load fees when applicable.

One notable difference that is less positive about bond funds is that your principal is not secured. With bonds, unless the company goes bankrupt, you will see your capital preserved, and in a U.S. government bond you will always see your capital retained.

The three primary types of bond funds are corporate, government, and municipal. You can also find global bond funds investing in markets worldwide, convertible bond funds, and closed-end bond funds. These funds will often be listed as short-term, intermediate, or long-term, giving you a choice. Often the longer-term bonds will fluctuate more and be more risky because of changes in the interest rate, while paying off higher yields.

Many people select bond funds to round out an equity fund portfolio, with perhaps two stock funds and two bond funds, or one balanced fund and one bond fund. Often the inclusion of a bond fund is to have a conservative safeguard in the portfolio.

chapter seven

Retirement Plans and Other Safe Investments

It's never too early to plan for your retirement or to set your sights on other future goals. As life expectancy increases, there are more years to enjoy, so it's to your benefit to plan accordingly. There are various popular options that provide comfortable investment opportunities. Some, like 401(k) plans are retirement plans set up by employers, while others, like IRAs, are retirement plans that you set up for yourself. These plans will work as a vehicle for various types of investments.

Along with, and included in, retirement plans are other investment options besides stocks, mutual funds, and bonds. CDs, for example, may not be generating the same excitement as the hottest stocks and mutual funds, but they serve very important purposes. They are short-term cash instruments that work for a conservative investor looking simply to keep some money in a safe place. Treasury instruments like T-bills (Treasury bills) provide an extremely safe haven for investors who are looking for a cash instrument and no fear that the "company"—or in this case the country—will go under.

401(k) Plans

For nearly 20 years, one of the most significant investing tools has been the 401(k) plan. Not actually an investment but a vehicle to invest within, the 401(k) is designed to help you save money (and build money) for retirement. The plan is set up by your employer and works in a manner similar to that of a mutual fund. These plans are becoming more and more common in major companies. The money is pooled and invested in stocks, bonds, mutual funds, or other types of investments. Usually the money is taken via salary reductions directly from your paycheck and goes directly into your 401(k) account. If such a plan is offered where you work, there is no reason not to jump at the opportunity. Putting the money in a plan earmarks it for your retirement, and you don't have to pay taxes on it as the money grows. AND, employers generally put in a contribution as well, which can be 10, 25, or even 50 percent of the amount you are contributing.

A 401(k) plan can be set up by an employer in a number of different manners, with some going into effect immediately and others kicking in after you've worked in the company for six months or even a year. Currently, as of 1999, you can contribute up to $10,000 of your salary to your 401(k) plan in a given year.

The big difference between a 401(k) and buying your own mutual funds is that you are not penalized if you sell your shares in a mutual fund, although you can lose money. In a 401(k), you must maintain the account until you are 59½ years old, or you will face a penalty upon early withdrawal.

Similar to mutual funds, your investment in a 401(k) is diversified, and you generally have several options as to where you want the contribution invested. Furthermore, you can change the percentage of money you want in a particular area. Plans generally invest in general growth funds, equity funds, money market accounts, and sometimes in shares of stock in your own company.

When you change jobs, by your own choice or by the decision of your company, you can have your 401(k) plan directly transferred to the new employer if they also offer such a retirement plan. By having the 401(k) rolled over by direct trustee to direct trustee, known as a trustee-to-trustee transfer, you will not have the money in your possession or personal account and will avoid paying taxes on it. By law, employers have to allow you to roll the money over. If you rollover the money yourself, the company will issue you a check for the money, less 20 percent, which they hold onto as insurance that you will roll it over into another 401(k) or into an IRA. You have to roll the money over in 60 days or you'll be hit with taxes and penalties, and you'll have to replace the 20 percent your company withheld.

With the 401(k) you can take your money out in one lump sum, which will mean paying taxes at one time. You can take the money out over time, spreading tax payments out, or roll the 401(k) into an IRA. Like an IRA, at 70 you must start taking money out or face penalties. However, if you are still working at 70, you can keep the money in the plan and keep contributing.

For people working in nonprofit organizations such as schools or hospitals, a 403(b) plan may be available, which works similarly to a 401(k). Such plans generally have fewer investment options, but they are also tax-deferred and similar in their makeup. Government workers may be offered a 457 plan, which is also similar in principle to a 401(k) or 403(b), with some additional restrictions.

IRAs

The most popular retirement plan of the last decade has certainly been the IRA, or Individual Retirement Account. Now sporting two varieties, IRAs offer you a safe tax-favored way for your money to grow for your retirement years.

Traditional IRAs

The traditional IRA allows you to contribute up to $2,000 per year, and contribute up to an additional $2,000 per year for a non-working spouse. A couple filing a joint tax return may put up to $4,000 into two separate IRA accounts, the only stipulation being that the amount being put into either account not exceed $2,000. If you are receiving alimony you also qualify to make an IRA contribution. All or a portion of your contributions may be tax-deductible, depending on your adjusted gross income (AGI) and whether or not you participate in a qualified retirement plan.

While you will be able to deduct all or part of your contributions into a traditional IRA, once there are earnings, they will compound annually, tax-free. Thus your account will grow more rapidly than if taxes were deducted. If you have many years ahead for your IRA account to grow until retirement, it is worthwhile to watch your money grow without taxation.

Of course, like anything else, IRAs have their rules, and a traditional IRA says once you put money in for retirement, it is there until you are 59½ years old. This essentially ensures that you are indeed putting the money away for retirement purposes (even if you keep on working past 59½). If you withdraw money prior to 59½, you will be penalized unless you qualify for one of a few exceptions, including first-time home-buying expenses, substantial medical costs, qualifying higher education expenses, or ongoing disabilities.

Once you are past 59½ years of age you can withdraw the money as you see fit until you are 70½, at which point the government starts putting minimums on how much you need to withdraw annually. When you do withdraw the money you will pay income taxes on the investment earnings based on your tax bracket. The long period of tax-deferred income, however, still outweighs this taxation. Also, it is very often the case that the income level for someone in their sixties, and perhaps semi-retired, is lower than it was in their forties, so they will fall into a lower tax bracket. Since the government changes the rules from time to time, and the methods of taxation in the United States are under a great deal of criticism, some experts feel that if you can defer tax payments for another 20 years, why not do so. After all, tax laws could certainly change by the second decade of the twenty-first century.

As for actually starting your IRA, you can choose to start one through a bank, brokerage house, or mutual fund depending on where you want your money to be invested. Traditionally banks offer fewer options than brokerage houses for where your IRA investment can go, usually sticking with the safer options such as a CD. Brokerage houses offer a wider range of options should you choose to be more savvy with your IRA investment, or you can play it safe with a money market fund. Mutual funds are, by definition, (usually) riskier than a CD or money market account. Essentially, within the IRA you need to do some investing homework if you want to get the most out of the account. The long time frame of an IRA makes equities or equity funds more attractive for some investors. Like other investments you can move your investments around within the IRA and suit your level of comfort in regard to risk.

Roth IRAs

The Roth IRA, named for legislation formulated by Senator William Roth, is a relatively new IRA that offers no tax deductions when you contribute at the same $2,000 annual ceiling, but (and this is the good part) upon withdrawal you will not be taxed. In fact, there are very few regulations when it comes to withdrawing the money from a Roth IRA. The money must be in the plan until you are at least 59½. However, the money can be withdrawn after five years, penalty-free, if you are disabled, if you use the distribution to pay up to $10,000 of the qualifying first-time home-buying expense, or if the distribution is to another beneficiary following the death of the account owner. If you do not need to take the money out, however (unlike a traditional IRA where at age 70½ the government says you must start making minimum withdrawals or face a penalty), you can leave the money in the Roth IRA with no minimum distributions upon withdrawal. This can even allow for a large tax-free benefit to pass directly to your heirs if you so choose.

For a Roth IRA, your income will determine your eligibility. This income structuring began with the advent of the new Roth IRA in 1998 and is subject to change, so you must ask about your eligibility when you decide to investigate a Roth IRA. As of 1999 the Roth is phased out as adjusted gross income (AGI) rises above $95,000 and $110,000 on a single return and between $150,000 and $160,000 on a joint return.

Which IRA Is Right for You?

Assuming you are eligible for both traditional and Roth IRAs, the biggest determining factor is whether it is to your benefit to take a deduction now and have to pay the taxes on withdrawing the money or to take no deduction at present and not have to worry about taxation or minimum deductions upon withdrawing the money later. The determination of whether to invest in or rollover your money from a traditional IRA to a Roth is based on your own financial situation. Many experts agree that taking the tax hit on the $2,000 now is far better than taking it on the much larger sum later on.

The bottom line is that no matter how much you calculate, you cannot know for sure what the next 30 years have in store in terms of taxes, the rate of inflation, the cost of living, your own health, and the stability of your job. While it is to your advantage to put money away for your retirement years, the decision to choose the traditional or the Roth IRA is not as tough as it is made out to be. Either way you will have saved money for your retirement years. If you qualify for both plans, the simple equation, as stated earlier, is whether it's to your benefit to take tax deductions now or whether you can afford not to and have benefits later on. Thus, figure out basic, approximate numbers with your accountant, consider other factors in your life, make an overall assessment of your future as you'd like it to be, and pick one.

Certificates of Deposit (CDs)

Unlike a 401(k) or an IRA, which are vehicles in which to place investments for retirement, a CD is a cash investment unto itself.

Through a bank or credit union you can purchase a CD for three months, six months, a year, or several years. Insured by the FDIC, these popular places to store your money have no risk. You can spend a few hundred or a few thousand dollars on a CD—banks usually set minimums. CDs secure an interest rate when you initially purchase them. Yields on CDs, while not matching those of the stock market, will generally run between 4 and 5 percent, which matches many bonds. Interest can be paid out to you periodically on longer-term CDs or paid to you all at once on shorter-term CDs (a three-month CD will pay upon maturity). Interest can, and often is, reinvested. You should also take note of how interest is paid out. You'll see interest compounded daily, weekly, monthly, and so on. This is as important as locking in a good interest rate. Since banks are no longer regulated, and can pay the interest that they set up, it's important that you lock in a good rate. While CDs are not bringing home the high returns they were in the 1980s, the rates are competitive, so you should shop around—read the ads and financial listings and check online for the best interest rate.

The one drawback of a CD is liquidity. If you need to cash in your CD early you will be penalized. It's often suggested that you divide your money up over several CDs purchased at different times and, therefore, with different maturities. This system of "laddering" will lock in better (and worse) interest rates, but will allow you to have CDs maturing at various times, should you need the cash. This does require good record keeping, especially if you are reinvesting once the CDs come due.

U.S. Treasury Bills

In the 1980s, T-bills—as U.S. treasury bills are known—were paying double-digit returns. Needless to say, they were very popular investments. Today, T-bills are not paying tremendous returns, but they are still very safe; like government bonds, they are backed by the full faith and credit of the United States government. Treasury bills are sold at government auctions every Monday. The government sets the yield price, which in recent years has been around 5 percent.

When you purchase a T-bill, through your bank or directly through the federal government, you immediately get a check for the amount at which the bill is paying interest. Therefore if you buy a $5,000 T-bill at 5 percent, you will receive a check for $250, or 5 percent, about a week after you've invested. If it's a 26-week T-bill you will then have a chance to renew at 26 weeks or get the $5,000 investment back. Every time you renew you get the interest check immediately, which is your "discount."

T-bills are good investments because they are safe and cannot be taxed at the local or state level, making them preferable if you live in a state that has high state taxes. Of late the rates have been low, but they have kept pace with most cash instruments. Your money, however, is not liquid, which often discourages people from long-term T-bills.

Until 1998, T-bills were sold in minimums of $10,000, which put them out of reach for many investors. Now they can be had for as little as $1,000 and purchased in increments of $1,000.

You can sell T-bills and notes based on the interest rate. If you have a long-term note with, for example, an 8 percent rate and other notes are paying 5 percent, you might want to sell it. Your $10,000 note could be worth $12,000 on the market. It's all a matter of supply and demand, and a high-yield note in a low-yield market is valuable. Of course, it can also go the other way. Your 5 percent bill could be worth far less if everyone else is able to buy bills at 8 percent. If you hold to maturity, however, you will get your initial investment or principal back.

Since there are no longer actual "certificates" issued, U.S. securities are issued in what is known as "book form," which means they are issued by electronic entries. Interest is paid into a treasury direct account, which you open when you purchase a U.S. treasury security from the Federal Reserve Bank. A broker can also purchase a U.S. treasury for you and set up your treasury direct account, but for this you will pay at least $50.00 for a service that you can easily do yourself. Call the Federal Reserve Bank closest to you and ask to set up an account.

Treasury notes come in either the two- and five-year variety, which are auctioned the last business day of the month, or the three- and 10-year notes, which are auctioned quarterly. For notes over five years the minimum investment is $1,000, but for five years or less the minimum is $5,000. You can purchase treasury notes from the U.S. government that range from one to 10 years. They are exempt from state and local taxes, which can make them appealing, and they are also safe investments backed by the full faith and credit of the U.S. government. The shorter-term notes, usually under four years, are sold for $5,000 or more, with the longer-term notes, four to 10 years, selling for $1,000+. Treasury notes have longer terms (one to 10 years) than T-bills. They pay interest semi-annually, whereas T-bills pay all your interest in one lump sum. The other advantage of treasury notes was, until last year, that they cost less than T-bills (T-bills had a $10,000 minimum), but T-bills can now be purchased for various amounts.

chapter eight

Investing and Taxes

Naturally, there's a fly in the ointment when you talk about those high returns that have been seen on fast-rising tech stocks and hot mutual funds. Once again, good old Uncle Sam wants a piece of the action. The primary areas of concern regarding taxes on investments are capital gains tax and tax on interest and dividend income

There are fine details and strategies you can discuss with your accountant regarding both of these areas. The bottom line, however, is that any interest or dividend income generated from your investments, unless you are in a tax-sheltered retirement plan such as a 401(k) or an IRA, will be taxed at your normal rate of return.

Capital gains, from selling your shares of stock, shares of a mutual fund, bonds, and so forth, are either considered short-term capital gains or long-term capital gains. If you held the investment for at least one year, it is considered a long-term capital gain (or loss). Most long-term capital gains are taxed at a maximum of 20 percent. Short-term gains are taxed at your rate of income tax. The profits on items or investments received via inheritance are also considered long-term capital gains.

What many investors fail to think about when they purchase a mutual fund is that all dividends or capital gains within the fund are taxable, even if they are then reinvested. Your statement will show how much your earnings were within that fund during the year, and they should indicate which were capital gains from the sale of a security and which earnings were interest income from dividends.

Zero coupon bonds will also be taxed even though you are not seeing any interest as your investment grows to full maturity. The interest is being reinvested and growing through compound interest. But as a $7,000 purchase in a "zero" grows to its full $20,000 value, you will be taxed each year on the portion of the $13,000 that has been earned.

Another area of confusion comes with treasuries or municipal bonds when they are sold on the secondary market. Once again, these tax-exempt bonds are taxable in this manner. Tax-exemption comes in the area of dividends and interest income and only where specified. For example, if you buy a tax-exempt municipal in another state it may be taxable (and usually is) in your state.

If you should lose money and have a capital loss, you can take up to $3,000 as a deduction and, if your loss was greater than $3,000, spread the remaining amount over several years. For example, if you lost $6,000, you could take a $3,000 deduction for one year and then take another one for the next year as well.

One of the most important concerns regarding taxation is record keeping. The basics of taxes and capital gains are relatively simple regarding the long term versus short term, the 20 percent ceiling on long-term gains, and declaring interest and dividends as income. The problems that arise are often due to dealing with more than one brokerage house, inheriting items, and other manners of having securities that are more complicated than a simple stock purchase at a broker (for which you have statements). If, for example, you transferred your account from one brokerage house to another, the new brokerage house will have a record of when you started dealing with them. If you changed brokers three months ago and you are doing your taxes, how do you report the capital gains on a stock you just sold that you actually owned for three years? It's a long-term capital gain and can be taxed at the 20 percent maximum. BUT, you have to show that you bought it three years ago and not simply look at the statement from the new brokerage house, which may only date back three months.

In short, you need to keep records of the buying and selling of all securities and at what cost. You should carefully file each transaction statement. When you inherit something of "value," get it appraised in writing. Once you have the fair market value, you can accurately report the capital gain should you sell it. The same holds true when you sell a collectible or artwork. The income must be reported and you should have a written record of the transaction. A paper trail of all transactions is VERY important should you ever be audited. One of the biggest difficulties people run into with the IRS is a lack of backup information. This also means it is your responsibility to make sure your broker is providing you with all the necessary paperwork.

Since taxes are part of almost all aspects of making money, they shouldn't deter you from investing as you so choose. You can help manage your tax risk by rounding out portions of your portfolio with tax-free investments. Naturally, in a retirement plan, these investments would be useless since you are already tax-deferred.

index

FIND MORE ON THIS TOPIC BY VISITING

BusinessTown.com
The Web s big site for growing businesses!

- ☑ **Separate channels on all aspects of starting and running a business**
- ☑ **Lots of info on how to do business online**
- ☑ **1,000+ pages of savvy business advice**
- ☑ **Complete web guide to thousands of useful business sites**
- ☑ **Free e-mail newsletter**
- ☑ **Question and answer forums, and more!**

businesstown.com

Accounting
Basic, Credit & Collections, Projections, Purchasing/Cost Control

Advertising
Magazine, Newspaper, Radio, Television, Yellow Pages

Business Opportunities
Ideas for New Businesses, Business for Sale, Franchises

Business Plans
Creating Plans & Business Strategies

Finance
Getting Money, Money Problem Solutions

Letters & Forms
Looking Professional, Sample Letters & Forms

Getting Started
Incorporating, Choosing a Legal Structure

Hiring & Firing
Finding the Right People, Legal Issues

Home Business
Home Business Ideas, Getting Started

Internet
Getting Online, Put Your Catalog on the Web

Legal Issues
Contracts, Copyrights, Patents, Trademarks

Managing a Small Business
Growth, Boosting Profits, Mistakes to Avoid, Competing with the Giants

Managing People
Communications, Compensation, Motivation, Reviews, Problem Employees

Marketing
Direct Mail, Marketing Plans, Strategies, Publicity, Trade Shows

Office Setup
Leasing, Equipment, Supplies

Presentations
Know Your Audience, Good Impression

Sales
Face to Face, Independent Reps, Telemarketing

Selling a Business
Finding Buyers, Setting a Price, Legal Issues

Taxes
Employee, Income, Sales, Property, Use

Time Management
Can You Really Manage Time?

Travel & Maps
Making Business Travel Fun

Valuing a Business
Simple Valuation Guidelines

visit the

fastread

Home Page at
www.fastread.com

Fastread.com is a new Web site designed to give you the information you need quickly. It covers subjects such as:

- ✦ Investing
- ✦ Personal Finance
- ✦ Getting out of Debt
- ✦ The Internet
- ✦ Building your own Home Page
- ✦ plus more to come!

If you want some tips or facts, and you want them fast, visit **fastread.com**. And remember, your time is money!

 FOR THOSE OF US WHO DON'T HAVE ALL DAY!